MASTERING THE GAME OF SUCCESS

How Game Theory and AI Are Redefining Business Strategies

CONSULTORIA IA

Copyright © 2024 CONSULTORIA IA

All rights reserved

The characters and events portrayed in this book are fictitious. Any similarity to real persons, living or dead, is coincidental and not intended by the author.

No part of this book may be reproduced, or stored in a retrieval system, or transmitted in any form or by any means, electronic, mechanical, photocopying, recording, or otherwise, without express written permission of the publisher.

Cover design by: Art Painter
Library of Congress Control Number: 2018675309
Printed in the United States of America

TO OUR FAMILY

CONTENTS

Title Page

Copyright

Dedication

Brief Review

Why read this book

Target audience

Preface

Chapter 1: The New Rules of the Game: How Game Theory Shapes Business Strategy

Chapter 2: AI as the Ultimate Game-Changer: Redefining Decision-Making in Business

Chapter 3: The Intersection of Game Theory and AI: Crafting Winning Strategies

Chapter 4: Outmaneuvering the Competition: Strategic Thinking in the Age of AI

Chapter 5: The Future of Business Strategy: AI, Game Theory, and Beyond

Appendices

BRIEF REVIEW

Mastering the Game of Success delves into the intersection of game theory and artificial intelligence, offering a fresh perspective on modern business strategies. This book explores how businesses can harness these powerful tools to outmaneuver competitors, optimize decision-making, and adapt to rapidly changing markets. Through practical insights and real-world examples, it reveals how AI and strategic thinking can work together to unlock new pathways to success, making it an essential guide for leaders aiming to thrive in the digital age.

WHY READ THIS BOOK

In an era where business environments are becoming increasingly complex and competitive, *Mastering the Game of Success* offers a roadmap for staying ahead. By blending game theory with cutting-edge AI insights, this book equips readers with the strategies to make smarter, more informed decisions, anticipate market shifts, and outmaneuver competitors. Whether you're a business leader, strategist, or entrepreneur, this book provides actionable tools to navigate uncertainty and thrive in the digital economy, making it essential for anyone aiming to future-proof their success.

TARGET AUDIENCE

The target audience for Mastering the Game of Success: How Game Theory and AI Are Redefining Business Strategies includes:

1. Business Leaders and Executives: Seeking innovative strategies to stay competitive in an AI-driven world.

2. Entrepreneurs: Looking to leverage advanced decision-making techniques to build resilient and successful businesses.

3. Strategists and Consultants: Interested in applying game theory and AI to solve complex business problems and optimize outcomes.

4. Tech and Innovation Enthusiasts: Curious about the practical applications of AI in transforming business landscapes.

5. Students and Academics: Studying business strategy, economics, AI, or game theory who want to explore cutting-edge approaches to business success.

6. Investors and Decision-Makers: Aiming to understand how AI and strategic thinking can influence market dynamics and business outcomes.

This book appeals to anyone keen on mastering future-forward strategies that blend technology with human insight.

PREFACE

In today's fast-paced, unpredictable business landscape, traditional strategies are no longer enough. The rise of artificial intelligence and data-driven decision-making is reshaping industries, and the future belongs to those who can adapt, innovate, and think strategically. As business becomes more complex, understanding the dynamics of competition, cooperation, and optimization has never been more crucial.

This book, *Mastering the Game of Success: How Game Theory and AI Are Redefining Business Strategies*, was born out of the desire to bridge the gap between two powerful tools: game theory and artificial intelligence. Individually, these concepts have already revolutionized the way companies operate, but when combined, they offer even greater potential. Game theory provides a framework for understanding the interactions between competitive agents, while AI empowers businesses to make faster, smarter decisions in real time.

Our goal is to make these concepts accessible to leaders, entrepreneurs, and decision-makers, whether you have a deep technical background or are simply looking for ways to future-proof your business. Through real-world case studies, practical applications, and actionable insights, we'll show how you can leverage AI and game theory to outmaneuver competitors, optimize your strategies, and thrive in an ever-changing digital world.

This book is not just a theoretical exploration; it's a guide designed to equip you with the tools you need to master your own game of success. Whether you're leading a startup, managing a multinational corporation, or simply seeking to understand the forces driving today's business environment, we hope you find the strategies and ideas presented here both enlightening and empowering.

Welcome to the future of business strategy.

CONSULTORIA IA

Sevilla, 2024

CHAPTER 1: THE NEW RULES OF THE GAME: HOW GAME THEORY SHAPES BUSINESS STRATEGY

In the fast-paced, ever-evolving landscape of modern business, success is no longer solely determined by intuition, experience, or the ability to make quick decisions. Today, businesses are increasingly embracing the principles of game theory—a field of study originally developed to understand strategic interactions in competitive environments. This shift has introduced a more analytical, structured approach to decision-making, where understanding the moves of competitors, customers, and even regulatory bodies is essential to achieving long-term success.

Game theory fundamentally revolves around one central concept: strategic interdependence. In a competitive marketplace, businesses are rarely acting in isolation. Every decision made by one firm—whether it's pricing, marketing, product development, or entering new markets—impacts others. In turn, the reactions of competitors and other stakeholders impact the original decision-maker. It's a perpetual, interconnected cycle of action and reaction, where understanding and predicting the behaviors of others is vital.

Understanding the Fundamentals of Game Theory

At its core, game theory is the mathematical study of conflict and cooperation. It provides a framework for anticipating the actions of others in strategic settings and making decisions that optimize outcomes for all involved. While its origins can be traced back to the 1940s with John von Neumann and Oskar Morgenstern's groundbreaking work, "Theory of Games and Economic Behavior," game theory has since expanded to cover a wide range of applications across economics, political science, and business.

To understand how game theory influences modern business strategy, it's essential to grasp some foundational concepts:

1. Players: In game theory, "players" are decision-makers, whether individuals, businesses, or other entities. In the business context, players could be companies competing within the same market, supply chain partners, customers, or regulatory bodies.

2. Strategies: A strategy is a course of action a player may take. In business, strategies are often complex and can involve various combinations of pricing, marketing tactics, research and development efforts, and negotiations. The key is that players must anticipate the strategies of others and decide their course of action accordingly.

3. Payoffs: The outcomes of strategies are measured in terms of "payoffs," which could be profits, market share, or other key performance indicators. The goal in any game is to maximize one's payoff while considering how competitors' decisions will impact those outcomes.

4. Nash Equilibrium: One of the most famous concepts in game theory is the Nash equilibrium, named after mathematician John Nash. A Nash equilibrium occurs when players choose the best possible strategy, given the strategies chosen by others. No player can improve their payoff by unilaterally changing their strategy. In business, this concept can be applied to pricing wars, product launches, or even negotiations where each side arrives at a stable, mutually beneficial outcome.

5. Zero-Sum vs. Non-Zero-Sum Games: In zero-sum games, one player's gain is another player's loss, such as a company gaining market share at the expense of a competitor. In non-zero-sum games, it's possible for all players to benefit, creating win-win situations. Non-zero-sum games are more common in business settings, where cooperation and competition often coexist. Think of joint ventures, partnerships, or cross-industry collaborations that benefit multiple parties.

Applying Game Theory to Business Strategy

In today's hyper-competitive environment, business leaders are increasingly recognizing the value of game theory in shaping strategies that are both resilient and adaptive. While traditional strategy models focus heavily on internal resources and market positioning, game theory emphasizes the importance of anticipating competitor moves, understanding incentives, and creating strategies that optimize interactions with other players in the market.

1. Competitive Dynamics: Outmaneuvering Rivals

One of the most obvious applications of game theory is in competitive strategy. In industries where a few dominant players control the market—think of tech giants like Apple, Google, or Amazon—understanding competitor behavior is crucial. Game theory enables firms to predict the reactions of competitors to their strategic moves and adjust their actions accordingly.

Consider a classic example of pricing strategy. In markets with price-sensitive consumers, lowering prices can lead to higher market share, but it may also provoke price cuts from competitors, leading to a price war. Using game theory, businesses can simulate various pricing scenarios, anticipating how competitors might react and determining whether initiating a price cut will lead to a favorable Nash equilibrium or a destructive race to the bottom.

Additionally, businesses can use mixed strategies—where a company randomizes between different strategies to keep competitors off balance. In the context of pricing or marketing, adopting a mixed strategy can prevent competitors from predicting moves with certainty, thereby gaining a competitive edge.

2. Cooperative Game Theory: Building Alliances and Partnerships

Not all business interactions are adversarial. Cooperative game theory focuses on scenarios where collaboration can lead to mutual benefits. In the world of modern business, partnerships, mergers, and joint ventures are increasingly common as companies look to leverage complementary strengths to achieve shared objectives.

For example, consider the technology and automotive industries. Companies like Tesla and Toyota have partnered with technology firms like NVIDIA and Google to develop autonomous driving systems. In these scenarios, game theory helps businesses evaluate the optimal terms for partnerships, ensuring that the distribution of benefits is fair and that all parties are incentivized to cooperate effectively.

Another common application of cooperative game theory is in supply chain management. Large firms like Walmart or Amazon rely on a network of suppliers, logistics providers, and distributors to deliver products efficiently. By applying game theory, these firms can optimize their relationships, ensuring that each partner is motivated to contribute to the overall success of the supply chain without taking advantage of others.

3. Decision-Making Under Uncertainty: Embracing Strategic Risk

Business leaders often face high levels of uncertainty, whether it's due to changing market conditions, regulatory shifts, or technological disruptions. Game theory offers a structured approach to making decisions under uncertainty, enabling companies to weigh the risks and rewards of different strategic moves.

A key concept in this context is minimax strategy—a decision-making rule that minimizes the maximum potential loss. In highly uncertain markets, this conservative approach can prevent catastrophic outcomes. However, game theory also supports more aggressive strategies, where companies embrace calculated risks in pursuit of higher rewards.

The rise of artificial intelligence (AI) is further enhancing game theory's application in decision-making under uncertainty. AI-powered models can analyze vast amounts of data, identifying patterns and predicting competitor behaviors with increasing accuracy. This enables businesses to refine their strategies in real-time, adapting quickly to new market conditions and maintaining a competitive edge.

How AI Is Revolutionizing Game Theory in Business

The intersection of game theory and AI represents a powerful frontier in business strategy. AI systems excel at processing large datasets and running simulations, making them ideal for analyzing complex, multi-player games that are typical in competitive industries.

For instance, AI can enhance auction theory—a subset of game theory used in pricing and bidding strategies. Online advertising platforms like Google and Facebook use real-time auctions to determine which ads are shown to which users. Through machine learning algorithms, these platforms can analyze millions of bids in real time, optimizing ad placements for both advertisers and the platform itself.

AI is transforming repeated games, where the same players interact over time, and past actions influence future strategies. Companies that engage in long-term contracts or recurring negotiations can use AI to track competitor behaviors over time, uncovering patterns that inform better strategies. This dynamic approach allows businesses to refine their decision-making continuously, rather than relying solely on static models.

Mastering the Game of Success

Game theory is no longer a theoretical exercise reserved for economists and mathematicians. In today's interconnected, competitive world, its principles are shaping how businesses design strategies, make decisions, and interact with competitors, partners, and customers.

The rules of the game are constantly evolving, and mastering these rules requires not only a deep understanding of the market but also the ability to anticipate and respond to the moves of others. As businesses continue to embrace game theory—and with the increasing integration of AI into these processes—the potential to optimize outcomes, maximize payoffs, and drive success will only grow.

Business leaders who can apply the principles of game theory effectively will have a powerful tool in their arsenal, enabling them to navigate the complexities of the modern market and position their companies for long-term success. In the coming chapters, we will delve deeper into how specific game theory concepts, such as signaling, commitment, and bargaining, can be leveraged to refine business strategies and win in the marketplace.

Key Concepts: Nash Equilibrium, Zero-Sum Games, and Competitive Advantage

In the dynamic landscape of business strategy, game theory provides a structured approach to understanding and predicting how companies, competitors, and other stakeholders will behave in complex and competitive environments. By applying the foundational concepts of Nash equilibrium, zero-sum games, and competitive advantage, companies can better anticipate market movements, make informed decisions, and ultimately gain a lasting edge over their rivals.

Nash Equilibrium: Stability Amidst Competition

The Nash equilibrium is one of the most influential concepts in game theory, named after mathematician John Nash. It describes a situation in which, given the strategies of all other players, no single player can improve their payoff by unilaterally changing their strategy. In essence, each player's decision is optimal in response to the decisions of others, creating a stable outcome where no one has an incentive to deviate.

In the context of business strategy, Nash equilibrium helps firms understand the importance of strategic balance. Each firm must consider the actions of competitors, partners, and consumers before deciding on its course of action. In competitive markets, companies often arrive at Nash equilibria without explicit coordination—rather, it results from the strategic interplay of independent decision-making.

Example: The Prisoner's Dilemma in Pricing Wars

One of the most famous applications of Nash equilibrium is in the prisoner's dilemma. Imagine two competing firms, A and B, in the same industry, both trying to maximize profits. Each firm can choose to lower prices (aggressive pricing) to attract customers or maintain high prices (cooperative pricing). If both firms maintain high prices, they maximize their collective profits, dividing the market equally. However, if one firm lowers prices while the other maintains high prices, the price-cutting firm gains a larger market share, increasing its profit at the other's expense. If both firms lower prices, a price war ensues, leading to lower profits for both.

In this case, the Nash equilibrium occurs when both firms choose to lower prices. While they would be better off collectively maintaining high prices, each firm fears that the other might undercut them, so both act in their own self-interest. This mutual suspicion and anticipation lead to a stable, though suboptimal, outcome for both firms.

Real-world example: Consider the airline industry, where price wars are common. Two major airlines operating on the same routes might face the temptation to cut ticket prices to attract more passengers. If one airline drops its prices, the other must follow suit to remain competitive. This tit-for-tat behavior drives prices down, sometimes below profitable levels, resulting in thinner margins for both airlines. The Nash equilibrium in this scenario is a form of strategic standoff where neither airline can raise prices without risking market share loss, and neither can drop prices too much without damaging profits. Therefore, they often settle into a competitive equilibrium where prices are low but stable.

Example: The Technology Industry and Platform Competition

Nash equilibrium is also critical in industries where network effects are at play, such as the technology sector. Take the case of competing digital platforms like Apple iOS and Google Android. Both companies must decide how much to invest in app developer ecosystems, with the goal of attracting more users and developers to their platform.

If both Apple and Google invest heavily, they may maintain a balance of power, each continuing to attract users and developers. If one chooses not to invest, it risks losing users to the competitor's platform, as users prefer platforms with a wider variety of apps and better functionality. In this scenario, the Nash equilibrium occurs when both companies invest heavily in their ecosystems. Neither can afford to reduce investment without risking a significant loss of market share to the other.

Zero-Sum Games: Winners and Losers in Competitive Markets

A zero-sum game is a situation where one player's gain is another player's loss. In these games, the total payoff remains constant, meaning that whatever one player wins, the other player loses an equivalent amount. Zero-sum games are often used to describe highly competitive markets where companies vie for a fixed pool of customers or resources, and one company's success directly comes at the expense of others.

In the business world, while zero-sum games can certainly occur, many competitive situations are non-zero-sum, meaning that cooperation or innovation can grow the total market, benefiting multiple players simultaneously. However, understanding the dynamics of zero-sum games remains crucial for industries where competition is fierce and resources are limited.

Example: The Sports Industry and Zero-Sum Outcomes

Professional sports leagues often operate under zero-sum conditions. In sports, each game has a clear winner and a loser—one team's victory is the other's defeat. Similarly, in industries tied to sports, such as sports apparel or broadcasting rights, companies can experience zero-sum competition. For example, Nike and Adidas compete fiercely for athlete endorsements and sponsorship deals. If Nike secures a deal with a star athlete, Adidas loses out on that opportunity, and vice versa.

This competition extends to market share as well. If Nike captures a larger share of the market for basketball shoes, Adidas inevitably loses share in that same segment. The combined market size may remain relatively fixed, meaning that one brand's gain represents the other's loss.

Example: The Energy Industry and Fossil Fuels

The energy sector is another industry where zero-sum dynamics frequently come into play. For instance, consider the competition between traditional fossil fuel companies and renewable energy firms. Governments, consumers, and businesses must allocate their resources between fossil fuels and renewable energy investments. As governments around the world increase their focus on renewable energy policies, subsidies for fossil fuel companies may be reduced, shrinking the overall pie for the traditional energy sector.

In this case, the market for energy can be viewed as a zero-sum game where each investment in renewable energy represents a loss for fossil fuel producers. While this is a simplified example, it illustrates the inherent competitive tension between two industries vying for the same pool of customers and resources.

Competitive Advantage: Winning in the Game of Business

Game theory is not just about predicting competitor behavior; it's also about crafting strategies that secure a competitive advantage. A competitive advantage occurs when a firm is able to perform better than its rivals, often through superior products, services, innovation, or cost structures. Applying game theory enables businesses to identify opportunities for gaining this advantage by exploiting strategic gaps and outmaneuvering competitors.

In markets where competition is intense, achieving competitive advantage requires firms to not only react to competitor actions but also anticipate future market changes and act proactively.

Example: Amazon's Long-Term Strategy

Amazon is a prime example of a company that has leveraged game theory principles to maintain a competitive advantage. Early in its development, Amazon recognized that its primary competitors in the retail space were constrained by the need for physical stores. Instead of competing head-to-head with traditional retailers, Amazon focused on building an expansive online infrastructure, drastically reducing costs and improving customer convenience.

By prioritizing scale, Amazon created a massive logistics network that allows it to offer faster delivery times and a broader range of products than most competitors. This strategic foresight gave Amazon a first-mover advantage, enabling it to dominate the online retail market. Competitors like Walmart and Target have since invested heavily in e-commerce, but Amazon's early adoption of digital infrastructure gives it a lasting edge.

Amazon also employs mixed strategies by continually innovating across multiple business lines, from cloud computing (Amazon Web Services) to entertainment (Amazon Prime Video). This diversification not only reduces its dependence on retail but also creates multiple avenues for growth, further solidifying its competitive advantage. Through game theory, Amazon has been able to strategically balance competition and cooperation, partnering with businesses in some areas while outcompeting them in others.

Example: Apple's Innovation Strategy and Ecosystem Control

Apple's competitive advantage comes from its ability to control its ecosystem. By designing both hardware and software in-house, Apple ensures that its products work seamlessly together, creating a "walled garden" that encourages customer loyalty. Game theory plays a crucial role in Apple's strategy, as the company anticipates the moves of competitors and customers.

For example, Apple's decision to control the entire value chain—rather than outsourcing production or relying on external software developers—gives it the flexibility to quickly adapt to market changes without being constrained by external dependencies. By anticipating the importance of customer data privacy, Apple also positioned itself as a leader in security, further distinguishing its products from those of competitors like Samsung or Huawei.

Apple's competitors, on the other hand, have struggled to match the company's level of integration, often relying on fragmented ecosystems of hardware manufacturers and software developers. This has led to a strategic Nash equilibrium in the smartphone market where Apple maintains a premium segment of the market, while Android-based manufacturers focus on lower-cost alternatives. Apple's competitive advantage lies not in dominating the entire market but in owning a highly profitable niche, where customer loyalty and ecosystem lock-in create significant barriers to entry for competitors.

Real-World Examples of Game Theory in Action

The principles of game theory are constantly at play in the business world, shaping everything from pricing strategies to corporate negotiations and beyond.

Example: The Airline Industry and Pricing Strategy

As previously mentioned, the airline industry frequently sees the application of game theory in the form of pricing strategies. Airlines must carefully balance the need to attract passengers with the need to maintain profitability. If one airline lowers ticket prices, competitors are often forced to follow suit, leading to a price war that reduces margins for everyone. However, if all airlines maintain high prices, they risk losing customers to

new market entrants offering cheaper alternatives. The result is a delicate equilibrium, where airlines constantly monitor each other's pricing strategies and adjust their own to stay competitive.

Example: The Telecommunications Industry and Spectrum Auctions

Telecommunications companies around the world use game theory to bid on spectrum licenses, which are necessary for offering mobile services. Governments often hold auctions to allocate spectrum, and companies must carefully consider their bids. Bidding too high may secure a valuable license but could hurt the company's financial position. Bidding too low, on the other hand, risks losing the license to a competitor. Game theory helps companies model the likely behavior of competitors, allowing them to determine optimal bidding strategies.

Real-world example: In the United States, the Federal Communications Commission (FCC) frequently holds spectrum auctions, where major telecommunications players like Verizon, AT&T, and T-Mobile bid against each other for spectrum bands. These auctions are highly competitive, with billions of dollars at stake. Companies must use game theory to anticipate how much their competitors are willing to bid, balancing the need to win valuable spectrum with the risk of overpaying.

Example: The Pharmaceutical Industry and Patent Races

In the pharmaceutical industry, companies engage in patent races to be the first to develop and market new drugs. The first company to secure a patent gains a significant competitive advantage, as it can enjoy monopoly profits for the duration of the patent period. However, the race to develop new drugs is fraught with risk, as research and development (R&D) costs are high, and there is no guarantee of success. Game theory helps pharmaceutical companies decide how much to invest in R&D, taking into account the likelihood of success and the potential actions of competitors.

Real-world example: The race to develop a COVID-19 vaccine is a prime example of game theory in action. Pharmaceutical companies like Pfizer, Moderna, and AstraZeneca invested billions of dollars in vaccine research, knowing that the first to market would reap substantial rewards. At the same time, companies had to weigh the risks of failure, as unsuccessful vaccine candidates would result in massive financial losses. In the end, multiple companies succeeded in developing vaccines, but each had to carefully balance the risks and rewards of their R&D investments.

Game Theory as a Strategic Tool

Game theory is a powerful tool for businesses navigating competitive landscapes. By understanding key concepts like Nash equilibrium, zero-sum games, and competitive advantage, companies can better anticipate competitor behavior, craft winning strategies, and achieve long-term success. Whether through pricing strategies, innovation, or market positioning, game theory provides a framework for making strategic decisions that balance risk and reward, cooperation and competition.

As industries continue to evolve, the principles of game theory will remain relevant, offering businesses a structured approach to navigating the complexities of modern markets. Whether competing in high-tech sectors, traditional industries, or emerging markets, companies that understand and apply game theory are more likely to gain a sustainable edge in the game of business.

Industry/Context	Game Theory Application	Key Concept	Statistical Data (Hypothetical)
Airline Industry	Pricing strategies based on competitors' actions	Nash equilibrium, zero-sum game	- Average price reduction after competitor lowers prices: 5%-10% - Market share increase after price cut: 2%-4%
Telecommunications	Spectrum auctions and bidding strategies	Auction theory, competitive advantage	- Average bid increase in final auction rounds: 15%-20% - Auction success rate for top 3 companies: 80%
Pharmaceutical Industry	Patent races for developing new drugs (e.g., COVID-19 vaccines)	Patent race, R&D investment strategy	- Success rate for major pharmaceutical R&D projects: 10%-20% - Investment cost per project: $1B - $2B
Tech Industry	Pricing models for software and hardware (e.g., smartphones)	Price wars, strategic pricing	- Revenue loss per price war: 5%-15% - Time spent at breakeven before price recovery: 6-12 months

| Retail Industry | Competitive pricing and product differentiation | First-mover advantage, product pricing | - Average price reduction due to competitor actions: 5%-8%
- Market share increase after product differentiation: 3%-5% |

Summary Table

CHAPTER 2: AI AS THE ULTIMATE GAME-CHANGER: REDEFINING DECISION-MAKING IN BUSINESS

Artificial intelligence (AI) is increasingly recognized as the ultimate game-changer in modern business strategy. In the same way that game theory revolutionized decision-making by providing a structured approach to competitive situations, AI is now taking this evolution several steps further. AI not only provides the framework for decision-making but also enhances it by analyzing vast amounts of data, predicting outcomes, and suggesting optimal strategies. It enables businesses to operate with a level of precision, speed, and insight that was unimaginable just a few decades ago. For decision-makers, this means a fundamental shift in how they approach problems, opportunities, and competition.

In this chapter, we will explore how AI transforms decision-making processes in business, offering not only increased efficiency and accuracy but also a redefinition of what it means to make a strategic decision in a complex, fast-moving marketplace. The implications of AI in decision-making are profound, and businesses that harness this potential are positioning themselves to thrive in the competitive environments of the future.

The Evolution from Intuition to Data-Driven Decisions

Traditionally, decision-making in business has been heavily reliant on human intuition, experience, and sometimes, gut instinct. Senior leaders often leveraged their past experiences and personal insights to guide their organizations, especially when navigating uncertainty. While experience is invaluable, this intuitive approach to decision-making is often limited by cognitive biases, incomplete information, and the inability to process complex data. In today's fast-paced business environment, relying solely on intuition is becoming increasingly insufficient.

AI has fundamentally changed this paradigm by offering a data-driven, analytical approach to decision-making. Modern AI systems can analyze enormous amounts of structured and unstructured data, identifying patterns, correlations, and insights that may elude even the most experienced executives. These systems do not simply process data; they understand it in ways that allow businesses to make more informed, precise, and objective decisions.

For example, consider the retail industry, where decision-making has historically been influenced by trends, seasonality, and customer feedback. AI can now analyze point-of-sale data, customer reviews, social media mentions, and weather patterns to forecast demand with remarkable accuracy. This allows companies to optimize inventory, adjust marketing strategies, and even personalize customer interactions in real-time. AI not only augments decision-making capabilities but also enables businesses to respond to shifts in market dynamics faster than ever before.

Automating Routine Decisions

One of the most immediate ways AI transforms decision-making is by automating routine and repetitive tasks. In the past, many business decisions—especially operational ones—required significant human input, even when the decisions were relatively straightforward. AI changes this by automating these processes, freeing up human talent to focus on more strategic and high-value tasks.

Take supply chain management as an example. Managing the flow of goods, materials, and services across multiple locations and stakeholders requires a myriad of decisions, many of which involve complex variables like demand forecasting, inventory management, supplier coordination, and logistics. Traditionally, supply chain managers would need to manually assess these variables to make decisions, often leading to inefficiencies and delays.

AI-driven systems can now handle these tasks by continuously analyzing real-time data from various sources, such as suppliers, weather conditions, transportation networks, and market demand. These systems can make decisions—such as rerouting shipments, adjusting inventory levels, or identifying the optimal supplier—far faster than humans, all while considering more variables than any human could process simultaneously. By automating these routine decisions, AI not only saves time but also reduces the risk of human error, leading to more efficient operations and cost savings.

However, AI is not merely about automating routine decisions. Its real power lies in its ability to enhance and redefine more complex, strategic decisions.

Enhancing Strategic Decision-Making with Predictive Analytics

Strategic decision-making is inherently more complex than routine operational choices. It involves multiple stakeholders, long-term implications, and significant uncertainty. This is where AI shines brightest, using predictive analytics and machine learning algorithms to help leaders make more informed strategic choices.

Predictive analytics leverages AI to forecast future trends, identify emerging opportunities, and anticipate risks. Unlike traditional forecasting methods that rely on historical data and human judgment, AI-based predictive models use sophisticated algorithms that learn from past data and adapt as new data becomes available. These models are not static; they evolve, making them far more accurate and insightful over time.

In industries like finance, predictive analytics has become indispensable. Financial institutions use AI to analyze market trends, customer behavior, and macroeconomic indicators to make better investment decisions. These AI systems can predict stock price movements, identify potential market disruptions, and even recommend portfolio adjustments based on a deep understanding of market dynamics.

In other sectors, such as healthcare, AI-driven predictive analytics is helping hospitals and medical providers anticipate patient needs, optimize resource allocation, and even predict outbreaks of diseases. The ability to forecast future scenarios allows businesses and organizations to make proactive, rather than reactive, decisions, positioning them to seize opportunities and mitigate risks before they fully materialize.

AI can simulate different decision outcomes using what-if scenarios. This capability allows decision-makers to explore various possibilities and their implications, testing strategies before committing to a specific course of action. By modeling the impact of different choices, businesses can avoid costly mistakes and maximize their chances of success.

Reducing Cognitive Bias in Decision-Making

Human decision-making is often influenced by cognitive biases—systematic patterns of deviation from rationality that can lead to suboptimal decisions. These biases include confirmation bias (favoring information that supports pre-existing beliefs), anchoring bias (relying too heavily on the first piece of information encountered), and availability bias (overestimating the importance of information that is easily recalled). In business, cognitive biases can have significant consequences, leading to poor investment decisions, flawed marketing strategies, and misguided hiring practices.

AI offers a solution to this problem by providing objective, data-driven insights that are not influenced by human biases. Because AI systems rely on algorithms and data rather than subjective judgment, they can help organizations make more rational and evidence-based decisions.

For instance, in hiring and recruitment, AI-powered tools can screen job candidates more objectively by focusing on qualifications and experience rather than personal biases that may affect human interviewers. AI systems can analyze resumes, assess skills, and even conduct initial interviews using natural language processing, all while eliminating factors like gender, race, or age that might unconsciously influence a human decision-maker.

Similarly, in marketing, AI helps eliminate biases by analyzing customer behavior data without preconceived notions. AI can segment customers based on actual behaviors rather than assumptions, allowing companies to target their campaigns more effectively. This not only enhances decision-making but also fosters greater inclusivity and diversity in business practices.

Real-Time Decision-Making in a Dynamic World

The pace of business today requires companies to make decisions in real-time or near real-time, especially in industries like finance, retail, and technology. This is another area where AI excels, as it can process and analyze vast amounts of data in real-time, providing decision-makers with the information they need to respond instantly to changing conditions.

Consider the world of high-frequency trading in financial markets. In this highly competitive space, decisions must be made in milliseconds to take advantage of market fluctuations. AI-driven trading algorithms can analyze market data, execute trades, and adjust strategies in real-time, far faster than any human could. These systems are designed to adapt to market conditions, constantly learning and optimizing their performance to maximize returns.

In customer service, AI-powered chatbots and virtual assistants can make real-time decisions by responding to customer inquiries, troubleshooting issues, and even processing transactions instantaneously. This not only improves customer satisfaction but also allows companies to handle higher volumes of interactions without the need for additional human resources.

The ability to make decisions in real-time is crucial in today's fast-moving business environment. AI enables businesses to stay agile, react to disruptions, and capitalize on fleeting opportunities that might otherwise be missed.

AI-Driven Decision-Making in a Competitive Landscape

In an increasingly competitive global market, the businesses that succeed will be those that make faster, smarter, and more strategic decisions than their competitors. AI gives companies the edge by transforming decision-making into a more scientific, data-driven process.

For example, in the manufacturing sector, AI is used to optimize production schedules, predict equipment failures, and manage supply chains more efficiently than ever before. Predictive maintenance, powered by AI, allows manufacturers to identify potential issues in machinery before they lead to costly downtime. This not only improves operational efficiency but also provides a competitive advantage by reducing production costs and increasing output.

In the retail space, AI helps companies anticipate customer preferences, optimize pricing strategies, and tailor marketing efforts to individual consumers. By understanding consumer behavior at a granular level, AI allows retailers to make decisions that drive sales and enhance customer loyalty.

In the tech sector, AI enables companies to innovate faster by automating research and development processes. AI-driven systems can analyze patent data, market trends, and customer feedback to identify potential areas for innovation. This accelerates the product development cycle, allowing companies to bring new products to market more quickly than their competitors.

The use of AI in decision-making is no longer a luxury but a necessity for businesses that want to maintain a competitive edge. Those that fail to embrace AI risk being left behind in an increasingly data-driven world.

The Human-AI Partnership in Decision-Making

Despite AI's impressive capabilities, it is important to recognize that AI is not a replacement for human decision-making but rather an enhancement. The most effective decisions are made when humans and AI work together, combining the best of both worlds—AI's analytical power and humans' creativity, intuition, and ethical judgment.

AI can process vast amounts of data and identify patterns that humans might miss, but it lacks the ability to understand context, empathize with customers, or navigate the complexities of human relationships. Human decision-makers, on the other hand, bring emotional intelligence, strategic vision, and the ability to consider broader societal and ethical implications. Together, they form a powerful partnership that allows businesses to make smarter, more balanced decisions.

As AI continues to evolve, the role of human decision-makers will shift from making routine decisions to overseeing and guiding AI systems. Human leaders will need to develop new skills, such as data literacy, critical thinking, and the ability to interpret AI-generated insights. By working alongside AI, humans can focus on higher-level strategic thinking, innovation, and leadership, while AI handles the heavy lifting of data analysis and routine decision-making.

The Future of AI-Driven Decision-Making

AI is not just transforming decision-making in business—it is redefining it. By automating routine tasks, enhancing strategic decisions with predictive analytics, reducing cognitive biases, and enabling real-time responses, AI offers businesses unprecedented levels of insight, speed, and precision. However, the true power of AI lies in its ability to augment human decision-making, allowing businesses to operate at a higher level of efficiency and competitiveness.

As AI continues to advance, the businesses that embrace its potential will not only make better decisions but will also lead the way in shaping the future of their industries. Those that resist this transformation may find themselves struggling to keep up in a rapidly evolving marketplace. The future of decision-making in business is here, and AI is at its forefront.

Predictive Analytics, Machine Learning, and Optimization: Integrating AI into Your Business Strategy for Competitive Advantage

The world of business is changing rapidly, and at the heart of this transformation is artificial intelligence (AI). Specifically, the integration of predictive analytics, machine learning, and optimization techniques into business strategies is emerging as a crucial factor for competitive advantage. In this chapter, we will explore how these technologies work, how they can be applied across industries, and how they empower businesses to make smarter, faster, and more strategic decisions. We will dive into the real-world applications and provide rich examples of how companies have successfully integrated AI into their operations, creating tangible benefits such as improved efficiency, increased revenue, and enhanced customer satisfaction.

Predictive Analytics: Anticipating the Future with Data

Predictive analytics is the use of data, statistical algorithms, and machine learning techniques to identify the likelihood of future outcomes based on historical data. It goes beyond merely describing what has happened in the past; it predicts what is likely to happen in the future. For businesses, predictive analytics is a game-changer because it allows leaders to make proactive decisions rather than reactive ones.

Consider the retail industry. Companies like Amazon and Walmart use predictive analytics to forecast customer demand, allowing them to optimize inventory levels and reduce stockouts or overstock situations. By analyzing customer purchasing behavior, seasonal trends, and even external factors like weather patterns, these retailers can anticipate which products will be in high demand and ensure they are adequately stocked. This not only improves customer satisfaction but also reduces carrying costs and maximizes sales.

A powerful example of predictive analytics in action is seen in the airline industry. Airlines like Delta and Southwest use predictive analytics to forecast flight delays, identify maintenance issues, and optimize pricing. By analyzing data from past flights, weather conditions, and real-time aircraft performance, these companies can predict when a plane is likely to experience mechanical issues, allowing them to perform preemptive maintenance and avoid costly delays. Furthermore, predictive analytics helps airlines adjust ticket prices dynamically based on demand forecasts, maximizing revenue while offering competitive prices to customers.

The healthcare sector is another area where predictive analytics is making a significant impact. Hospitals and healthcare providers use predictive models to anticipate patient needs, optimize staff schedules, and reduce readmission rates. By analyzing patient data—such as medical history, lifestyle factors, and demographic information—hospitals can predict which patients are at high risk of developing complications or requiring additional care. This enables healthcare providers to intervene early, improving patient outcomes while reducing costs.

At its core, predictive analytics allows businesses to use data as a crystal ball, providing insights into what is likely to happen and empowering leaders to take action before problems arise or opportunities are missed.

Machine Learning: Powering Predictive Models and Continuous Improvement

Machine learning (ML) is a subset of AI that involves the development of algorithms that allow computers to learn from and make predictions based on data. Unlike traditional programming, where rules and logic are explicitly defined, machine learning models are designed to improve over time as they are exposed to more data. This makes machine learning particularly powerful in business applications, where conditions are constantly changing and decision-making must adapt accordingly.

A prominent example of machine learning in action is in the finance industry. Companies like JPMorgan Chase and Goldman Sachs use machine learning algorithms to detect fraud, analyze market trends, and improve customer experiences. For instance, fraud detection models analyze thousands of transactions in real-time, flagging any anomalies that may indicate fraudulent activity. These models continuously learn from new data, improving their accuracy in detecting suspicious transactions while minimizing false positives. This allows financial institutions to protect their customers while maintaining operational efficiency.

Machine learning also plays a significant role in the marketing and advertising space. Platforms like Google and Facebook use ML algorithms to optimize ad targeting, ensuring that businesses can reach the right audience at the right time. By analyzing user behavior—such as browsing history, search queries, and social media interactions—machine learning models predict which ads are most likely to resonate with specific individuals. This not only improves the effectiveness of advertising campaigns but also enhances the customer experience by delivering more relevant and personalized content.

In the automotive industry, machine learning is revolutionizing the development of autonomous vehicles. Companies like Tesla and Waymo use ML models to analyze data from sensors, cameras, and radar systems, enabling self-driving cars to make real-time decisions on the road. These models continuously learn from new driving experiences, improving their ability to navigate complex traffic scenarios, avoid obstacles, and ensure passenger safety. As machine learning models become more sophisticated, autonomous vehicles are expected to become safer and more efficient than human-driven cars.

One of the key advantages of machine learning is its ability to adapt and improve over time. Unlike traditional models, which may become outdated as conditions change, machine learning algorithms evolve by continuously learning from new data. This makes them highly effective in dynamic business environments where decision-making must be agile and responsive to change.

Optimization: Maximizing Efficiency and Value

Optimization is the process of finding the best possible solution to a problem, given a set of constraints and objectives. In business, optimization is used to maximize efficiency, minimize costs, and improve outcomes across various operations, from supply chain management to marketing strategies.

One of the most well-known examples of optimization in business is the use of algorithms to manage supply chains. Companies like Procter & Gamble and Unilever use AI-powered optimization models to streamline their supply chain operations, reducing costs and improving delivery times. By analyzing data on supplier performance, transportation costs, and inventory levels, these models identify the most efficient routes for shipping goods, the optimal reorder points for inventory, and the best suppliers for specific materials. This not only improves the speed and reliability of deliveries but also reduces waste and enhances profitability.

In the manufacturing sector, optimization is critical for improving production processes and minimizing downtime. Factories use optimization algorithms to schedule machine maintenance, allocate resources, and manage production lines. For example, General Electric (GE) uses AI to optimize its manufacturing processes, ensuring that its factories operate at peak efficiency. By analyzing data from sensors on machines, AI models can predict when equipment is likely to fail and schedule maintenance accordingly, reducing the risk of costly breakdowns and production delays.

In the world of logistics, companies like UPS and FedEx use optimization models to plan delivery routes, ensuring that packages are delivered in the most efficient and cost-effective manner possible. By analyzing traffic patterns, weather conditions, and delivery schedules, these models determine the optimal routes for drivers, reducing fuel consumption, cutting delivery times, and improving customer satisfaction. This level of optimization has become increasingly important in the era of e-commerce, where customers expect fast and reliable deliveries.

Optimization also plays a crucial role in the energy industry. Companies like Siemens and Schneider Electric use AI-powered optimization models to manage power grids and reduce energy consumption. These models analyze data from sensors, weather forecasts, and energy demand to optimize the distribution of electricity across regions. By ensuring that energy is allocated efficiently, these companies can reduce waste, lower costs, and minimize the environmental impact of energy production.

In marketing, optimization algorithms help companies allocate their advertising budgets more effectively. By analyzing data on customer behavior, conversion rates, and campaign performance, AI models can determine the optimal mix of channels, ad formats, and messaging to maximize return on investment. This allows businesses to get the most value out of their marketing spend while reaching their target audience more efficiently.

Integrating AI into Your Business Strategy for Competitive Advantage

The integration of AI into business strategy is not just about adopting new technologies; it's about reshaping the way businesses operate and compete. Companies that successfully leverage predictive analytics, machine learning, and optimization gain a significant edge over their competitors by making faster, more informed decisions and by continuously improving their operations.

The first step in integrating AI into a business strategy is identifying the areas where AI can deliver the most value. This often involves looking at existing processes that are data-intensive, time-consuming, or prone to errors. For example, industries that rely heavily on forecasting—such as retail, finance, and manufacturing—are prime candidates for predictive analytics. Companies that handle large volumes of customer interactions, such as telecommunications or e-commerce, can benefit from machine learning to improve personalization and customer service. And businesses with complex supply chains or production processes can use optimization algorithms to enhance efficiency and reduce costs.

Once potential areas for AI integration have been identified, the next step is to gather and structure the data needed to train AI models. AI relies on large amounts of high-quality data to function effectively, so businesses must invest in data collection and management. This often involves integrating data from multiple sources, such as internal databases, customer interactions, and third-party providers, into a centralized platform that can be used to feed AI models.

For example, Coca-Cola has integrated AI into its business strategy by using predictive analytics to forecast demand for its products. By analyzing data from sales, weather patterns, and customer preferences, Coca-Cola can predict which products will be in demand at specific times and in particular regions. This allows the company to optimize its supply chain, ensuring that the right products are in the right place at the right time. In addition to improving operational efficiency, this also helps Coca-Cola reduce waste and maximize sales.

Another critical component of AI integration is ensuring that the organization has the right talent in place to manage and leverage AI technologies. This may involve hiring data scientists, AI engineers, and other specialized roles or partnering with AI service providers to implement and maintain AI systems. It also means fostering a culture of innovation, where employees are encouraged to embrace AI and experiment with new ways of using it to solve business problems.

Take the example of Netflix, a company that has fully integrated AI into its core business strategy. Netflix uses machine learning algorithms to analyze viewer behavior and make personalized recommendations for what to watch next. By continuously learning from user interactions, these algorithms improve over time, delivering more accurate and relevant suggestions. This personalization has been a key driver of Netflix's success, increasing viewer engagement and retention, which ultimately translates into higher revenue. Netflix uses predictive analytics to forecast which types of original content will perform well with its audience, guiding its investments in new shows and movies.

One of the key challenges in integrating AI into a business strategy is ensuring that AI models are transparent and explainable. Decision-makers need to understand how AI models arrive at their conclusions, especially when those models are used to make critical decisions, such as approving loans, hiring employees, or diagnosing medical conditions. Ensuring transparency and interpretability is crucial not only for building trust in AI but also for ensuring compliance with regulations and ethical standards.

Lastly, businesses must recognize that integrating AI into their strategy is an ongoing process. AI models need to be continuously monitored, updated, and refined to ensure that they remain accurate and effective as conditions change. This requires a commitment to ongoing investment in AI technology and talent, as well as a willingness to adapt and evolve the business strategy as new AI capabilities emerge.

Achieving Competitive Advantage with AI

Predictive analytics, machine learning, and optimization are not just technological advancements; they are fundamental shifts in how businesses operate, make decisions, and compete. Companies that successfully integrate AI into their business strategies gain a significant advantage by making smarter, faster, and more efficient decisions than their competitors. By leveraging AI, businesses can anticipate future trends, optimize their operations, and deliver more personalized experiences to their customers. As AI continues to evolve, the businesses that embrace it will be the ones that lead their industries and shape the future of commerce.

It's important to remember that AI is not a one-size-fits-all solution. The key to success lies in identifying the right use cases for AI within the specific context of the business, gathering and managing the necessary data, and ensuring that the organization has the talent and infrastructure to support AI initiatives. By taking a strategic, thoughtful approach to AI integration, businesses can unlock new levels of efficiency, innovation, and competitive advantage, positioning themselves for long-term success in an increasingly data-driven world.

AI Technology	Description	Applications	Statistical Data	Impact on Business
Predictive Analytics	Utilizes historical data, statistical algorithms, and machine learning to predict future events and trends.	Retail (Amazon, Walmart), Airlines (Delta), Healthcare	Retail: 20-30% inventory reduction with predictive analytics Healthcare: 17% reduction in readmission rates	**Proactive Decision-Making**: Anticipates customer demand, optimizes inventory, reduces delays, improves patient outcomes, enhances efficiency.
Machine Learning	AI models that improve over time by learning from data. Powers systems to make predictions, detect patterns, and provide insights.	Finance (fraud detection at JPMorgan), Marketing (Google, FB)	Fraud detection: 10% annual fraud reduction in financial institutions Ad performance: 25% increase in ad conversion	**Continuous Improvement**: Learns from new data, identifies fraud, enhances personalization, improves customer experiences, optimizes marketing.
Optimization	AI techniques that find the best solutions within constraints to maximize	Supply Chains (Unilever, P&G), Manufacturing (GE), Logistics	Supply chain: 15-25% reduction in logistics costs Manufacturing: 10-15% production	**Operational Efficiency**: Optimizes resource allocation, reduces waste,

	outcomes like cost reduction, efficiency, and speed.		*efficiency improvement*	enhances manufacturing output, lowers logistics costs, improves delivery times.
AI Integration Strategy	Embedding AI (predictive analytics, ML, optimization) into business strategies to enhance decision-making and gain competitive advantage.	Cross-industry (Netflix, Coca-Cola)	*Personalization at Netflix: 75% of viewed content influenced by AI-driven recommendations Sales forecasting: 20%+*	**Competitive Advantage**: Personalized customer experiences, better demand forecasting, optimized supply chain operations, improved product targeting, faster decision-making, and proactive responses to market trends.
Data Requirements	High-quality, structured data necessary for AI models to perform effectively. Centralized data platforms integrate internal and external	Cross-industry (telecom, e-commerce)	*AI model accuracy: 80-90% depending on data quality*	**Enhanced Data Utilization**: AI-driven companies that invest in proper data management see improvements in predictions and decision-making accuracy,

	sources.			leading to enhanced operational performance and customer satisfaction.
Talent and Infrastructure	Requires hiring data scientists, AI engineers, and fostering a culture of innovation. Investment in infrastructure for AI implementation and continuous use.	Cross-industry (Tesla, Waymo for autonomous vehicles)	*Companies with AI talent see 25%+ improvement in data-driven decision-making*	**Ongoing AI Support**: AI implementation requires investment in talent and infrastructure to ensure long-term success. Businesses that hire the right expertise and nurture AI-driven cultures gain operational efficiencies and innovation.
Transparency & Ethics	Ensures AI models are explainable, transparent, and compliant with regulations. Critical for trust-building, especially in finance, healthcare, and	Cross-industry (financial services, healthcare, HR)	*90% of executives believe AI explainability is crucial for adoption*	**Trust and Compliance**: AI transparency leads to greater regulatory compliance, higher user trust, and better business outcomes in sectors requiring explainable models, such as

	hiring.			finance, legal, and healthcare.
Ongoing Monitoring	Continuous improvement of AI models is required as data evolves. Updating and refining AI models ensures relevance and accuracy.	Cross-industry (Netflix, autonomous vehicles)	*AI models improve by 5-10% per year with ongoing learning*	**Adaptability**: AI's ability to evolve ensures businesses remain competitive by consistently improving operations and adjusting to market trends.

Summary Table

CHAPTER 3: THE INTERSECTION OF GAME THEORY AND AI: CRAFTING WINNING STRATEGIES

In today's rapidly evolving business landscape, the need for smarter strategies is more pressing than ever. The intersection of game theory and artificial intelligence (AI) offers a powerful toolkit for crafting winning strategies that are both adaptive and effective in complex, dynamic environments. Game theory, the study of strategic decision-making in situations of competition and cooperation, provides the theoretical framework for understanding how rational actors make choices. AI, with its ability to process vast amounts of data and learn from it, brings automation, prediction, and optimization to the table. When combined, these two fields offer unprecedented opportunities to enhance decision-making, reduce uncertainty, and drive success across industries.

This chapter explores how businesses can leverage the synergy between game theory and AI to develop smarter, more effective strategies. From negotiations and pricing to competitive positioning and collaboration, the fusion of these disciplines is transforming how organizations approach strategic planning and execution. In the following sections, we will dive into the key principles of game theory, examine how AI enhances its applicability, and provide real-world examples of how this combination is being used to gain a competitive edge.

The Fundamentals of Game Theory: A Strategic Framework

Game theory is a mathematical approach to studying strategic interactions among individuals or entities that have competing or conflicting interests. Originating from the work of John von Neumann and Oskar Morgenstern in the mid-20th century, it has since become a vital tool in economics, political science, and, increasingly, in business strategy. At its core, game theory seeks to understand how rational actors behave in situations where the outcome depends not only on their own choices but also on the choices of others. This interdependence makes it particularly useful in competitive environments, where firms must constantly anticipate and respond to the moves of their rivals.

One of the key concepts in game theory is the "game," which refers to any situation where players (which could be individuals, organizations, or even algorithms) make decisions that affect each other. A game consists of players, strategies, and payoffs. Players choose strategies that maximize their payoffs, given the strategies chosen by others. These games can be cooperative, where players work together to achieve a mutually beneficial outcome, or non-cooperative, where each player seeks to maximize their own benefit, often at the expense of others.

A common example of game theory in action is the "Prisoner's Dilemma," a situation in which two players must decide independently whether to cooperate or defect. The optimal outcome for both is to cooperate, but uncertainty about the other player's actions often leads to both players defecting, resulting in a suboptimal outcome. This dilemma illustrates the tension between individual rationality and collective benefit, a recurring theme in strategic decision-making.

In business, game theory helps leaders understand the competitive landscape and predict how competitors, customers, and other stakeholders will respond to their actions. By modeling interactions as games, businesses can identify optimal strategies, anticipate competitive moves, and make better decisions under uncertainty.

The Power of AI: Enhancing Strategic Decision-Making

While game theory provides a solid theoretical foundation, its practical application in real-world scenarios is often limited by the complexity of the calculations involved. This is where AI comes into play. AI, particularly in the form of machine learning (ML), allows businesses to process and analyze vast amounts of data, uncover patterns, and make predictions that would be impossible for humans to perform manually.

AI can augment game theory in several key ways. First, it can automate the process of identifying and analyzing strategic interactions, allowing for real-time decision-making in dynamic environments. In many industries, the pace of change is so rapid that traditional strategic planning methods are no longer sufficient. AI's ability to continuously learn and adapt makes it an ideal tool for navigating such uncertainty.

Second, AI can enhance the predictive power of game theory by incorporating large datasets and complex models that account for a wider range of variables and interactions. For example, in pricing strategies, AI can analyze consumer behavior, competitor pricing, and market conditions to determine the optimal price point in real time. This level of precision and speed is essential in highly competitive markets where small advantages can make a significant difference.

Third, AI's ability to simulate a variety of potential outcomes allows businesses to test different strategies and scenarios before implementing them in the real world. This is particularly useful in negotiations or competitive situations, where understanding the potential reactions of other players is critical. AI-driven simulations can model various game-theoretic scenarios, providing businesses with insights into the likely outcomes of different strategic choices.

Crafting Winning Strategies: A Synergistic Approach

The combination of game theory and AI offers businesses a powerful framework for crafting winning strategies. By integrating the theoretical rigor of game theory with the predictive and adaptive capabilities of AI, organizations can make more informed, data-driven decisions that increase their chances of success in complex, competitive environments.

One of the key advantages of this synergistic approach is the ability to optimize strategies in real time. Traditional strategic planning often relies on static models that are based on assumptions about the future. However, in a rapidly changing world, these assumptions can quickly become outdated. AI allows businesses to continuously update their models with new data, ensuring that their strategies remain relevant and effective.

For example, in the retail industry, companies like Amazon and Walmart use AI-powered pricing algorithms that continuously adjust prices based on demand, competitor actions, and other factors. By incorporating game-theoretic principles, these companies can anticipate how competitors will react to their pricing decisions and adjust accordingly. This not only helps them stay competitive but also ensures that they maximize profits while meeting customer expectations.

In the realm of negotiations, AI and game theory can work together to improve outcomes by analyzing the interests and potential moves of the other party. In complex negotiations, such as mergers and acquisitions or trade agreements, there are often multiple parties with conflicting interests. Game theory provides a framework for understanding these interactions, while AI can process vast amounts of data to identify patterns and predict the likely outcomes of different negotiation strategies. This combination allows businesses to negotiate more effectively, maximizing their chances of securing favorable deals.

Real-World Applications: Game Theory and AI in Action

The intersection of game theory and AI is already being leveraged by some of the most forward-thinking companies in the world. Below are a few examples of how this combination is being used to create smarter strategies across various industries.

1. Dynamic Pricing in E-commerce

As mentioned earlier, dynamic pricing is one of the most prominent applications of AI and game theory. Companies like Uber and Amazon use AI algorithms to adjust prices in real time based on a variety of factors, including demand, supply, and competitor behavior. Game theory comes into play when these companies must consider how their pricing decisions will affect their competitors and how their competitors' actions will, in turn, influence their own pricing strategies. By modeling these interactions as strategic games, companies can optimize their pricing to maximize revenue while staying competitive.

2. Autonomous Vehicles and Traffic Management

In the automotive industry, the development of autonomous vehicles relies heavily on game theory and AI. Self-driving cars must navigate complex environments where they must interact with other vehicles, pedestrians, and infrastructure. These interactions can be modeled as games, where each "player" (car, pedestrian, etc.) makes decisions based on their own goals and the expected behavior of others. AI allows autonomous vehicles to process real-time data from their surroundings and predict the actions of other players, enabling them to make safe, efficient decisions on the road.

Similarly, AI and game theory are being used to optimize traffic management systems in cities. By modeling traffic flow as a game, city planners can use AI to predict the impact of different interventions (e.g., changes in traffic light timings, road closures) on overall traffic patterns. This allows for more efficient management of urban transportation systems, reducing congestion and improving safety.

3. Supply Chain Optimization

In supply chain management, companies are increasingly using AI and game theory to optimize their operations. The global nature of modern supply chains means that businesses must constantly negotiate with suppliers, customers, and competitors to secure the best deals and ensure the timely delivery of goods. Game theory provides a framework for understanding these complex interactions, while AI can analyze data from across the supply chain to predict potential disruptions, identify opportunities for cost savings, and suggest optimal negotiation strategies. This combination helps businesses minimize risk and maximize efficiency in their supply chain operations.

4. Financial Markets and Trading

The financial industry has been one of the earliest adopters of AI, and game theory plays a critical role in shaping trading strategies. In financial markets, traders must constantly anticipate the actions of other market participants and adjust their strategies accordingly. Game theory provides a framework for understanding these strategic interactions, while AI allows traders to analyze vast amounts of market data in real time and identify patterns that would be impossible for humans to detect. This combination has led to the rise of algorithmic trading, where AI-powered systems execute trades based on game-theoretic models, often at speeds and scales that humans cannot match.

The Future of Game Theory and AI in Business Strategy

As AI continues to advance and game theory becomes more integrated into business decision-making, the potential for crafting even smarter, more effective strategies will only increase. The ability to anticipate competitors' moves, optimize operations in real time, and continuously adapt to changing conditions will be essential for businesses looking to stay ahead in an increasingly competitive global market.

One of the most exciting areas of development is the potential for AI and game theory to enhance collaboration. In many industries, the traditional focus on competition is giving way to a recognition that collaboration can often lead to better outcomes for all parties involved. By applying game-theoretic principles to collaborative situations, businesses can identify win-win strategies that benefit all stakeholders. AI can further enhance this process by analyzing data on past collaborations and predicting the likely outcomes of different partnership strategies.

The intersection of game theory and AI represents a powerful frontier in business strategy. By combining the theoretical insights of game theory with the computational power of AI, businesses can craft smarter, more adaptive strategies that give them a competitive edge in an increasingly complex world. Whether it's optimizing pricing, improving negotiation outcomes, or navigating complex supply chains, the integration of these two disciplines is reshaping the way organizations approach strategic decision-making. The future of business strategy lies at the intersection of game theory and AI, and those who can harness this synergy will be well-positioned to succeed in the years to come.

Case Studies of Businesses Using AI-Driven Game Theory Models

As technology continues to evolve at an unprecedented pace, businesses across various industries are increasingly adopting artificial intelligence (AI) to gain competitive advantages. Game theory, a discipline that focuses on strategic decision-making, has found new life when combined with AI's ability to process vast amounts of data and make predictive analyses. The integration of AI and game theory provides a rich framework that enables companies to not only predict competitor moves but also optimize their own strategies in dynamic, competitive environments. In this chapter, we will explore case studies that highlight how different businesses are successfully leveraging AI-driven game theory models to craft smarter strategies and drive success. Additionally, we will look at practical tools and frameworks for applying these concepts in real-world business settings.

Case Study 1: Amazon's Dynamic Pricing Strategy

Amazon is a leading example of a company that has successfully implemented AI-driven game theory models to optimize its pricing strategy. The e-commerce giant faces intense competition, not only from traditional brick-and-mortar retailers but also from other online platforms like Walmart, eBay, and Alibaba. To remain competitive, Amazon leverages AI-powered algorithms that adjust prices in real-time based on various factors, including demand fluctuations, competitor pricing, and consumer behavior.

AI-Driven Game Theory Application

Amazon's dynamic pricing system uses game-theoretic principles to anticipate how competitors might react to price changes. For example, when Amazon lowers the price of a popular item, it often triggers a response from competitors who may reduce their prices to maintain market share. Amazon's AI, however, is capable of analyzing these strategic interactions in real time. By doing so, it predicts how long competitors can sustain lower prices and adjusts Amazon's pricing accordingly to maximize profits while maintaining a competitive advantage.

A key feature of Amazon's pricing strategy is its ability to identify and exploit scenarios similar to the "Prisoner's Dilemma," a classic game theory problem where two competitors might both benefit from cooperating but end up defecting out of fear that the other will betray them. By lowering prices strategically, Amazon can force competitors into a suboptimal position where they either sacrifice profit margins to keep up or lose market share. Through continuous analysis and learning, the AI adjusts prices across millions of products daily, ensuring that Amazon remains a dominant player in the marketplace.

Results

The application of AI-driven game theory has been instrumental in making Amazon one of the most profitable e-commerce platforms in the world. By anticipating competitor moves and optimizing its own pricing strategies in real time, Amazon can maximize profitability without sacrificing its competitive position. This system has become a cornerstone of its broader strategy for staying ahead in a highly competitive market.

Case Study 2: Uber's Surge Pricing and Traffic Optimization

Uber is another example of a company that has successfully utilized AI-driven game theory to optimize its pricing model, particularly through its surge pricing mechanism. Surge pricing refers to the dynamic increase in ride prices during periods of high demand, such as rush hours or during special events. However, implementing surge pricing is more complex than simply increasing prices when demand spikes. The company must carefully consider both rider satisfaction and driver availability, as well as how competitors such as Lyft may respond to price hikes.

AI-Driven Game Theory Application

Uber's surge pricing algorithm incorporates game-theoretic principles to balance supply (drivers) and demand (riders) in real time. The system evaluates not only the current number of available drivers and ride requests but also the likely behavior of riders and drivers based on different pricing strategies. For instance, when prices increase due to surge conditions, some riders may opt to wait for prices to drop or switch to alternative transportation options. Similarly, drivers may be more willing to work during peak periods if they know that surge pricing is in effect, leading to an increased supply of available rides.

In addition to pricing, Uber's AI also models the behavior of competitors, such as Lyft, when implementing surge pricing. If Lyft does not match Uber's price surge, Uber risks losing customers who may prefer a cheaper ride. Thus, Uber must constantly balance pricing to ensure that it remains competitive while also optimizing its supply of drivers during high-demand periods. The AI system integrates real-time data from both internal sources (ride requests, driver locations) and external factors (competitor pricing, traffic conditions) to adjust surge pricing in real-time.

Results

By using AI-driven game theory, Uber has been able to implement a pricing strategy that maximizes both customer satisfaction and profitability. Surge pricing helps ensure that riders have access to rides during peak times, while drivers are incentivized to work when demand is highest. Additionally, Uber's ability to predict competitor behavior ensures that it remains competitive, even during high-demand periods. This dynamic, AI-powered approach to pricing has been a significant factor in Uber's continued growth and dominance in the ride-hailing industry.

Case Study 3: Alphabet's DeepMind and Energy Management

Alphabet's DeepMind, renowned for its breakthroughs in AI, has applied AI-driven game theory models in various sectors, including energy management. One of the most remarkable applications of this technology has been in optimizing the energy usage of data centers. These facilities consume vast amounts of electricity, and even small improvements in efficiency can lead to significant cost savings.

AI-Driven Game Theory Application

DeepMind used AI to model the energy consumption patterns of Google's data centers, identifying key variables that influenced energy use, such as temperature, server load, and cooling system efficiency. Game theory was applied to manage the trade-offs between different energy-saving strategies. For instance, cooling a data center during off-peak hours is cheaper than during peak hours, but delaying cooling can lead to overheating, which could affect server performance.

The AI-driven game theory model helped DeepMind strike the optimal balance between energy use and server performance by predicting the impact of different strategies and simulating possible outcomes. This model allowed Google to reduce its energy consumption by 40% without compromising data center performance. By continuously learning from the data, the AI system was able to adapt its strategies over time, leading to more refined and efficient energy management.

Results

The combination of AI and game theory enabled DeepMind to achieve remarkable results in energy efficiency. Google reported a 15% reduction in overall energy consumption and significant cost savings. This case study highlights the potential for AI-driven game theory models to optimize operational efficiency, particularly in industries where resource management is a critical factor.

Practical Tools and Frameworks for Applying AI-Driven Game Theory Models

The case studies above highlight the transformative potential of AI-driven game theory in various industries. However, for businesses looking to apply these concepts, it is essential to have practical tools and frameworks to guide their implementation. Below, we discuss several key approaches and tools that can help businesses leverage AI-driven game theory models effectively.

1. AI-Powered Strategic Decision Platforms

One of the most accessible ways for businesses to implement AI-driven game theory is through AI-powered strategic decision platforms. These platforms combine advanced analytics, machine learning, and game theory to help businesses simulate and model competitive interactions, customer behaviors, and market dynamics. Many of these platforms offer user-friendly interfaces that allow business leaders to input data and receive real-time insights without requiring deep technical expertise.

For example, platforms like Simudyne and Decision Lens allow companies to run simulations of competitive scenarios, such as pricing wars, product launches, or supply chain disruptions. By modeling different strategic decisions as games, businesses can test various outcomes and identify the optimal strategies. These platforms often integrate AI to analyze large datasets, enabling more accurate predictions and more nuanced decision-making.

2. Scenario Analysis Tools

Scenario analysis is a practical framework that allows businesses to explore different strategic options under uncertainty. In the context of AI-driven game theory, scenario analysis tools can help companies simulate various competitive dynamics and market conditions, providing a clear picture of how different strategies might play out in real-world situations.

For instance, a business might use scenario analysis to explore how changes in competitor pricing or market regulations could impact its market share. AI-driven tools like Crystal Ball or @Risk allow users to input a range of variables and run simulations based on game-theoretic models. These tools help businesses understand the potential risks and rewards associated with different strategic choices, allowing them to make more informed decisions.

3. Predictive Analytics with AI

Predictive analytics is a powerful tool for applying AI-driven game theory in business contexts. By analyzing historical data and identifying patterns, AI can predict how competitors, customers, or other stakeholders will behave in the future. For example, AI-driven tools like IBM Watson Analytics or SAS Analytics can analyze market trends, consumer behaviors, and competitor strategies to help businesses anticipate future developments and adjust their strategies accordingly.

By incorporating game theory into predictive models, businesses can simulate how different actors will respond to various strategic moves. This is particularly valuable in industries where competition is intense and small changes in strategy can have significant impacts on market position. For example, a company might use predictive analytics to anticipate how a competitor will respond to a new product launch or pricing change, allowing it to make preemptive moves that maximize its competitive advantage.

4. Negotiation Support Systems

In industries where negotiations play a crucial role, AI-driven game theory can be applied through negotiation support systems (NSS). These tools help businesses analyze the interests, objectives, and potential actions of negotiation partners, allowing them to identify the best strategies for reaching favorable agreements.

For example, Smartsettle Infinity is a negotiation support system that uses AI and game theory to optimize multi-party negotiations. The system models each party's objectives and constraints, simulates different negotiation strategies, and recommends the optimal approach. This is particularly useful in complex negotiations, such as mergers and acquisitions, where multiple stakeholders with conflicting interests must reach a consensus. By applying AI-driven game theory, businesses can negotiate more effectively and maximize their chances of securing a favorable outcome.

The intersection of AI and game theory offers businesses a powerful framework for crafting smarter, more effective strategies.

From dynamic pricing and traffic optimization to energy management and negotiation, AI-driven game theory models are helping companies navigate complex competitive landscapes with greater precision and confidence. By adopting practical tools and frameworks, businesses can harness the full potential of these models, gaining a competitive edge in an increasingly dynamic and uncertain world. Whether through strategic decision platforms, scenario analysis tools, or predictive analytics, the integration of AI and game theory is transforming the way businesses approach strategy and decision-making. Those that embrace this new paradigm will be well-positioned to succeed in the years to come.

CHAPTER 4: OUTMANEUVERING THE COMPETITION: STRATEGIC THINKING IN THE AGE OF AI

In today's hyper-competitive business world, the ability to outmaneuver competitors is a critical skill for any organization. While traditional strategies based on intuition and experience have always played a role, the rapid advancement of artificial intelligence (AI) and game theory has fundamentally redefined how businesses approach competition. These tools provide unparalleled insights into strategic decision-making, allowing companies to anticipate competitor moves, optimize their own actions, and create sustainable advantages in the marketplace.

Strategic thinking in the age of AI is more dynamic and complex than ever before. AI not only enhances data analysis and prediction capabilities but also creates entirely new dimensions of competition. By integrating game theory with AI, businesses can model interactions between competitors as if they were participants in a complex game, each seeking to maximize their own outcomes. Understanding these dynamics can help companies design strategies that account for not just their own actions, but also the likely responses of rivals, customers, and other stakeholders. This chapter delves into how AI and game theory can be used to outmaneuver the competition, redefining what it means to compete and win in today's business environment.

The Evolution of Competitive Strategy

Before exploring how AI and game theory are transforming competitive strategy, it's essential to understand the foundations of traditional strategic thinking. Historically, competitive strategy has been shaped by frameworks like Michael Porter's Five Forces, which helps businesses understand the forces shaping competition within an industry—rivalry among existing firms, the threat of new entrants, bargaining power of buyers, bargaining power of suppliers, and the threat of substitutes. These frameworks, while still valuable, are often static in nature and provide a snapshot of the competitive environment at a given point in time.

However, today's business landscape is not static—it's rapidly evolving. Industries are being disrupted by new technologies, customer preferences are changing, and global supply chains are becoming more complex. To keep up, businesses need to go beyond traditional strategic frameworks and adopt more dynamic approaches that can evolve as fast as the environment they operate in. This is where AI and game theory come into play.

Game Theory as a Blueprint for Strategy

Game theory, the study of strategic decision-making in situations where the outcome depends on the actions of multiple participants, provides a powerful framework for understanding competitive interactions. In business, competitors are not just passive actors; they are constantly making decisions that influence the market, whether it's launching a new product, changing pricing strategies, or forming partnerships. Game theory helps businesses model these interactions as a "game" where each player aims to achieve the best possible outcome given the decisions of others.

One of the key concepts in game theory is the Nash Equilibrium, named after mathematician John Nash. In this equilibrium, no player can improve their outcome by changing their strategy unilaterally, assuming the other players' strategies remain unchanged. This concept is crucial for businesses, as it helps them identify the point at which their competitors' strategies stabilize and what moves are optimal in response. However, while game theory has been a valuable tool in strategic planning for decades, its application was often limited by the complexity of real-world business interactions and the sheer volume of data required to model them accurately.

Enter AI. Artificial intelligence, with its advanced data processing capabilities and predictive algorithms, can now take game theory to a new level. AI systems can analyze vast amounts of data from multiple sources—competitor actions, market trends, customer behavior, and even social media—to identify patterns and predict how competitors might react in various scenarios. By combining AI with game theory, businesses can not only model competitive interactions more accurately but also develop more sophisticated strategies that adapt in real time to changes in the competitive landscape.

AI-Driven Decision Making: From Reactive to Proactive Strategies

One of the greatest strengths of AI is its ability to process and analyze massive amounts of data far more quickly and efficiently than any human could. This enables businesses to make data-driven decisions that are not only reactive but also proactive. Traditionally, many companies have relied on reactive strategies—responding to competitors' moves after they occur. While this approach can work in the short term, it often leaves businesses playing catch-up, particularly in fast-moving industries like technology and finance.

With AI, companies can shift from reactive to proactive strategies. Machine learning algorithms can detect subtle signals in the marketplace, such as shifts in consumer preferences or emerging competitive threats, before they become widely apparent. For example, AI might analyze customer sentiment data from social media to identify dissatisfaction with a competitor's product, providing an opportunity to launch a targeted marketing campaign or product improvement before the competitor has time to respond. Similarly, AI can help businesses anticipate competitor actions by analyzing historical data and detecting patterns that suggest a competitor is preparing to enter a new market or launch a price war.

These proactive strategies give businesses the ability to stay one step ahead of the competition. Rather than waiting to react to a competitor's move, companies can use AI to predict what their rivals are likely to do next and adjust their strategies accordingly. This level of foresight is invaluable in industries where the pace of change is accelerating and where even small competitive advantages can make the difference between success and failure.

Personalization at Scale: Leveraging AI to Outperform Competitors

One of the most powerful ways AI can help businesses outmaneuver the competition is through personalization at scale. In today's consumer-driven world, personalization has become a key differentiator. Customers expect products, services, and marketing to be tailored to their individual needs and preferences, and companies that can deliver personalized experiences have a significant competitive advantage.

AI allows businesses to deliver this kind of personalization at scale by analyzing customer data and developing highly targeted strategies. For example, AI can analyze purchasing behavior, online interactions, and demographic information to segment customers into highly specific groups and then deliver personalized marketing messages, product recommendations, and pricing strategies for each group. This level of personalization would be impossible to achieve manually, but with AI, it can be done efficiently and effectively, allowing companies to win over customers who might otherwise be drawn to competitors.

Moreover, AI-driven personalization goes beyond marketing. It can also be applied to product development, customer service, and supply chain management. By using AI to analyze customer feedback and preferences, businesses can develop products that better meet customer needs and adjust their supply chains to ensure those products are delivered quickly and cost-effectively. This not only improves customer satisfaction but also creates a barrier to entry for competitors who may not have the same level of insight into customer behavior.

The Role of Cooperation and Competition: A Balanced Approach

While AI and game theory are powerful tools for outmaneuvering the competition, it's important to recognize that not all business interactions are purely competitive. In many industries, businesses must strike a balance between competition and cooperation, a concept known as "coopetition." Coopetition occurs when companies that are competitors in some areas collaborate in others, such as in shared research and development initiatives or industry-wide standards-setting efforts.

Game theory provides valuable insights into how businesses can navigate this delicate balance. It helps companies understand when it's in their best interest to cooperate with competitors and when it's better to compete. AI, in turn, can enhance these insights by providing real-time data on competitor actions and market conditions, allowing businesses to adjust their strategies as needed.

For example, in industries like pharmaceuticals or technology, companies may collaborate on pre-competitive research to develop new technologies or treatments that benefit the entire industry. Once the foundational work is done, however, they shift to a competitive mode, each seeking to bring the best products to market. AI and game theory can help businesses navigate these transitions smoothly, ensuring that they maximize the benefits of cooperation while still maintaining a competitive edge.

Adapting to the Ethical and Regulatory Challenges of AI-Driven Competition

As AI becomes increasingly integrated into competitive strategies, businesses must also navigate the ethical and regulatory challenges that come with it. AI-driven decision-making raises important questions about transparency, fairness, and accountability. For example, if a company uses AI to predict competitor behavior and adjusts its pricing strategies accordingly, it could be accused of engaging in anti-competitive behavior, particularly if the AI's decisions are opaque and difficult to explain.

Regulators are beginning to pay more attention to how AI is used in business, and companies that fail to comply with evolving regulations risk fines, legal challenges, and damage to their reputations. To avoid these pitfalls, businesses must adopt ethical AI practices that prioritize transparency and fairness. This includes ensuring that AI algorithms are explainable and that decisions made by AI systems can be audited and justified. It also means being mindful of the broader social and economic impacts of AI-driven competition, such as the potential for AI to exacerbate inequality or displace jobs.

While these challenges are significant, they also present an opportunity for forward-thinking companies to differentiate themselves by adopting responsible AI practices. Companies that are proactive about addressing the ethical and regulatory challenges of AI will not only avoid potential pitfalls but also build trust with customers, regulators, and other stakeholders. In a world where trust is increasingly a competitive advantage, this can be a powerful differentiator.

Redefining Competitive Advantage in the Age of AI

As AI and game theory continue to evolve, they are fundamentally redefining what it means to compete and succeed in business. The companies that will thrive in the age of AI are those that embrace these tools not just as a way to optimize existing strategies, but as a way to develop entirely new approaches to competition.

Outmaneuvering the competition in this new landscape requires more than just reacting to the moves of rivals. It demands a proactive, data-driven approach that leverages AI to anticipate market trends, personalize customer experiences, and adapt strategies in real-time. By integrating game theory with AI, businesses can model complex competitive interactions and develop strategies that balance competition with cooperation, all while navigating the ethical and regulatory challenges of this new era.

In the end, mastering the game of success in the age of AI is about more than just winning—it's about continuously evolving and staying one step ahead in a world where the rules of the game are constantly changing. As AI continues to reshape the business world, the companies that can think strategically, adapt quickly, and execute effectively will be the ones that emerge as leaders in the new era of competition.

How to Anticipate Competitors' Moves Using Data-Driven Insights

In today's hyper-competitive business environment, anticipating competitors' moves is no longer just an advantage, it's a necessity. With advancements in artificial intelligence (AI) and the growing use of big data, companies have more tools at their disposal than ever before to gain a strategic edge. The ability to predict competitor behavior can shape critical business decisions and help organizations outmaneuver rivals. This section will delve into how businesses can leverage data-driven insights to anticipate competitors' moves and create more proactive strategies.

1. The Role of Predictive Analytics in Understanding Competitors

Predictive analytics has transformed the way businesses make decisions. By analyzing vast amounts of historical and real-time data, companies can now predict with considerable accuracy how their competitors might act in the future. Predictive models, powered by AI, can sift through data on competitor behavior, customer preferences, market trends, and economic indicators to identify patterns and signals that suggest upcoming strategies from competitors.

For example, retail giants like Amazon and Walmart use predictive analytics to anticipate the pricing strategies of competitors. By tracking competitors' historical pricing patterns, promotional calendars, and changes in product availability, these companies can adjust their prices dynamically, often undercutting rivals before they even have a chance to implement their new strategy. This kind of data-driven anticipation allows businesses to remain one step ahead, not just reacting to competitors but shaping the competitive landscape.

Moreover, predictive analytics can help companies foresee new market entrants. By monitoring venture capital trends, startup funding rounds, and technology developments, businesses can spot emerging competitors before they gain significant market share. This proactive approach to competition allows companies to prepare for and counteract potential disruptions in their industry.

2. Competitive Intelligence and Market Sensing

Competitive intelligence (CI) is the process of gathering and analyzing information about competitors, market conditions, and external factors that influence the competitive environment. With the influx of data available today, competitive intelligence has become more sophisticated and effective.

Companies can use web scraping tools and AI-driven data collection techniques to monitor competitor activities, such as new product launches, hiring patterns, patent filings, and even social media sentiment. For instance, if a competitor suddenly increases job postings for AI engineers, this could signal that they are planning to integrate AI into their product offerings. Similarly, tracking changes in patent filings or intellectual property applications can provide early warnings of new innovations that could disrupt the market.

An excellent example of competitive intelligence in action comes from the telecommunications industry. Large telecom companies frequently monitor the activities of smaller competitors to anticipate when new technology rollouts, such as 5G, are likely to happen. By gathering information on these smaller players' investment patterns, spectrum acquisitions, and collaborations with technology providers, major firms can anticipate the competitive moves and adjust their own rollout strategies to counteract them.

3. Scenario Planning and Game Theory in Competitive Strategy

Scenario planning is a powerful tool in anticipating competitor moves, especially when combined with game theory. Companies can use scenario planning to envision multiple potential futures based on competitor behavior, regulatory changes, and shifts in customer demand. By modeling different competitive scenarios, businesses can identify the most likely moves competitors will make under various conditions.

Game theory, in particular, allows companies to think through the possible strategies competitors might adopt. The theory assumes that competitors act rationally to maximize their own benefits, and it can be used to model interactions between firms in a given market. This approach is especially valuable in industries with a few dominant players, such as airlines, where the actions of one company directly influence the others.

For instance, in the airline industry, game theory models have been used to anticipate competitors' pricing strategies, route expansions, and even mergers and acquisitions. By anticipating how rivals will react to changes in ticket prices or the introduction of new routes, airlines can craft strategies that either preempt or counter those moves. By playing out various competitive scenarios and understanding the likely responses of competitors, companies can better prepare themselves for market shifts.

4. Using AI-Driven Sentiment Analysis to Gauge Competitor Strength

One of the emerging trends in data-driven insights is the use of sentiment analysis to gauge competitor strength and predict their next moves. AI-powered sentiment analysis tools can scan social media platforms, news outlets, and customer reviews to detect shifts in public perception of a company or brand.

For example, a sudden rise in positive sentiment around a competitor's new product launch might indicate a surge in demand, prompting a quicker response in terms of product upgrades, marketing, or pricing strategies. Conversely, a dip in sentiment around a competitor due to poor customer service reviews or a product recall could signal an opportunity for your company to capitalize on their misstep by ramping up your own marketing efforts.

Tech companies frequently use sentiment analysis to monitor competitors' standing in the public eye. For instance, a large-scale analysis of Twitter and Facebook posts can reveal growing dissatisfaction with a competitor's product. Armed with this information, companies can seize the opportunity to launch aggressive marketing campaigns, offering alternatives or discounts, effectively diverting customers away from the competitor during a vulnerable time.

Building Resilience and Adaptability into Your Strategies

Resilience and adaptability have become crucial components of strategic planning in the modern business landscape. While anticipating competitors' moves is essential, building strategies that are resilient and adaptable ensures that companies can weather unexpected disruptions, whether they come from competitors, economic shifts, or technological changes.

1. Fostering Agility through Modular Strategies

One of the most effective ways to build resilience is by creating modular strategies. Modular strategies break down large, overarching business goals into smaller, flexible components that can be adjusted independently. This approach enables a company to pivot quickly in response to external changes without overhauling its entire strategy.

For example, a company that adopts a modular approach to product development may roll out features in stages, allowing it to adjust based on market reception, competitor responses, or technological advancements. Tech companies like Apple and Google frequently use this approach, releasing beta versions or minimum viable products (MVPs) before the full-scale launch. This flexibility ensures that they can make changes in response to customer feedback or competitor innovations without derailing their long-term strategy.

2. Adopting a Data-Driven Feedback Loop

Resilient strategies are those that incorporate a continuous feedback loop, allowing companies to constantly refine their approach. By integrating real-time data collection and analysis into the decision-making process, businesses can ensure that they remain adaptable to changing market conditions.

For instance, companies can use A/B testing, customer surveys, and performance analytics to gather feedback on their products or services. By analyzing this data regularly, companies can identify shifts in customer preferences or market trends early and make adjustments before competitors have the chance to capitalize on the change. This approach fosters a culture of continuous improvement, where strategies are not static but evolve in real-time.

A real-world example of this can be seen in the e-commerce space, where companies like Netflix and Amazon constantly refine their recommendations algorithms based on customer viewing or purchasing habits. This adaptability ensures that they remain competitive, even as customer preferences and market dynamics shift.

3. Preparing for Black Swan Events with Stress Testing

Black swan events—unforeseeable disruptions like pandemics or natural disasters—can cripple businesses that are not prepared. To build resilience, companies should engage in stress testing their strategies against these extreme scenarios. Stress testing involves creating hypothetical scenarios that challenge the organization's assumptions and require it to respond under high-pressure conditions.

For example, during the COVID-19 pandemic, businesses that had conducted stress tests for supply chain disruptions were better equipped to pivot quickly. Companies like Tesla, which diversified its supply chain and integrated more flexible manufacturing processes, were able to resume production faster than competitors who had not anticipated such widespread disruptions. Stress testing not only helps build resilience but also fosters a mindset of proactive risk management.

4. Diversifying Revenue Streams for Long-Term Stability

Another crucial element of resilience is revenue diversification. Companies that rely on a single product, service, or market are vulnerable to disruptions in that area. By diversifying revenue streams, businesses can mitigate the risks associated with economic downturns, shifts in customer demand, or competitor encroachment.

Take the example of Google, which started primarily as a search engine but has since diversified into advertising, cloud computing, hardware, and AI services. This diversification has made Google more resilient in the face of challenges like changes in advertising regulations or competition from other search engines. A diversified strategy ensures that even if one area of the business faces challenges, other revenue streams can support the company.

Incorporating data-driven insights and building resilience into business strategies are not just advantageous but necessary for thriving in the modern, AI-driven competitive landscape. By leveraging predictive analytics, competitive intelligence, game theory, and stress testing, businesses can not only anticipate competitors' moves but also ensure that their strategies are adaptable and resilient in the face of unexpected changes. The ability to outmaneuver competitors requires foresight, flexibility, and a commitment to continuously refining and evolving strategies to stay ahead of the curve.

Key Strategy	Tools/Methods	Purpose	Examples/Industries	Expected Outcomes
Predictive Analytics	AI, Machine Learning, Big Data	Anticipate competitors' actions based on historical data	Retail (e.g., Amazon, Walmart)	Dynamic pricing, proactive strategy adjustments
Competitive Intelligence	Web Scraping, AI Data Collection, Social Media Monitoring	Gather insights on competitors' product launches, hiring, patents	Telecom (e.g., 5G rollout monitoring)	Preemptive actions, early detection of market trends
Scenario Planning & Game Theory	Modeling, Game Theory Analysis	Simulate competitor behavior under different market scenarios	Airlines, Technology	Strategic foresight, minimizing market risks
AI-Driven Sentiment Analysis	Sentiment Tracking Tools, Social Media Monitoring	Assess public perception shifts towards competitors	Tech companies, Consumer Goods (e.g., Apple, Google)	Exploit competitor weaknesses, quick response strategies

Modular Strategies	Incremental Development, MVP Testing	Enable fast pivoting in response to competitor moves	Tech (e.g., Google's phased product rollouts)	Increased flexibility, reduced risk
Data-Driven Feedback Loop	A/B Testing, Real-Time Analytics	Continuous improvement based on real-time data	E-commerce (e.g., Netflix, Amazon)	Enhanced adaptability, rapid adjustment to market trends
Stress Testing for Black Swan Events	Hypothetical Scenario Modeling	Prepare for unpredictable, high-impact disruptions	Manufacturing, Supply Chain (e.g., Tesla)	Increased resilience, faster recovery from disruptions
Revenue Diversification	Expansion into Multiple Markets or Products	Reduce reliance on single revenue source, mitigate risks	Tech Giants (e.g., Google)	Long-term stability, reduced risk from market shifts

Summary Table

CHAPTER 5: THE FUTURE OF BUSINESS STRATEGY: AI, GAME THEORY, AND BEYOND

In the modern business landscape, traditional strategies are no longer enough to secure competitive advantages or ensure long-term success. As markets evolve, so too must the approaches that guide companies through the complexities of global competition. At the heart of this evolution lies the powerful intersection of two revolutionary forces: Artificial Intelligence (AI) and game theory. Together, they are not merely transforming the way businesses think about strategy; they are redefining the entire playing field. AI and game theory—once separate disciplines—are converging to create strategies that are not only more predictive but also more adaptable, dynamic, and precise than anything the business world has seen before.

The evolving role of AI in shaping future markets is profound. While game theory provides the strategic frameworks that help businesses understand competitive dynamics, AI offers the computational power and machine learning algorithms to make those frameworks actionable in real-time. This combination is already influencing industries from finance to retail, healthcare to manufacturing, and this trend is set to accelerate. To grasp the future of business strategy, it's essential to explore how AI and game theory are converging, how they're transforming market behavior, and what businesses can do to position themselves for success in this rapidly changing environment.

The Strategic Shift from Human to AI Decision-Making

For much of business history, strategy was driven by human intuition, experience, and decision-making. CEOs and executives relied on a mix of data analysis, industry insights, and gut feelings to formulate strategies that would steer their organizations. While this worked in relatively static and predictable markets, today's business environment is anything but stable. Globalization, digital transformation, and disruptive technologies have made markets more complex, dynamic, and interconnected than ever before.

AI steps into this environment as a game-changer, providing unprecedented capabilities to process vast amounts of data, learn from it, and offer strategic recommendations that are far beyond human capacity. What makes AI so powerful in the context of business strategy is not just its ability to automate routine tasks, but its potential to augment decision-making by identifying patterns and predicting outcomes with incredible accuracy.

In the past, game theory models relied on human input to define the rules of competition, analyze potential moves by competitors, and suggest optimal strategies. These models were powerful, but limited by the scope of human calculation. AI, on the other hand, can process thousands of variables in real time, simulating multiple scenarios and outcomes. It can quickly update its understanding as new information becomes available, making AI-driven strategies more flexible and responsive to changes in the market.

Consider the use of AI in financial markets, where machine learning algorithms now predict stock prices, manage portfolios, and execute trades autonomously. These systems don't just react to the market—they actively anticipate moves based on historical data and patterns that human analysts might miss. Similarly, in retail, AI is being used to optimize pricing strategies, supply chain management, and customer experience. Retailers like Amazon and Alibaba have leveraged AI to predict customer demand, adjust prices in real-time, and personalize shopping experiences on an individual level. These capabilities go far beyond what traditional human-driven strategies could achieve, and they offer a glimpse into how AI will continue to reshape business strategy across all sectors.[1]

Game Theory and AI: A New Strategic Partnership

Game theory, which has long been used to model competitive interactions in business, is increasingly being integrated with AI to create more sophisticated strategic tools. In essence, game theory provides the "rules of the game," helping companies understand the strategic moves of competitors, partners, and stakeholders. AI, meanwhile, enhances the ability to simulate these interactions at scale, identifying optimal strategies not just for current conditions but for a range of possible future scenarios.

One of the most important contributions of game theory is its focus on interdependence. In business, the actions of one player (a company) often depend on the actions of another (a competitor, customer, or regulator). Game theory helps businesses anticipate the moves of others, identify potential areas of collaboration or conflict, and design strategies that maximize their own advantage while mitigating risks. For example, in the telecommunications industry, companies have long used game theory to make decisions about pricing, market entry, and network investments, considering not just their own positions but the likely responses of competitors.

Now, with the integration of AI, these game-theoretic models can become even more precise and actionable. AI can analyze massive datasets—such as consumer behavior, competitor actions, and market trends—and use this information to feed into game theory models, refining them in real-time. This allows businesses to move beyond static, one-time decisions and adopt strategies that evolve continuously as market conditions change.

A prime example of this can be seen in the tech industry, where giants like Google, Apple, and Microsoft use AI-driven game theory models to manage their competitive interactions. These companies compete fiercely in areas like cloud computing, artificial intelligence, and hardware development, but they also collaborate in areas where it benefits them, such as industry standards and regulatory lobbying. AI helps these companies navigate the complex interplay of competition and cooperation, identifying opportunities to outmaneuver rivals while avoiding destructive conflicts that could harm the overall ecosystem.

Real-Time Decision-Making: The New Norm

One of the most profound changes AI brings to business strategy is the ability to make real-time decisions. Traditional strategic planning often involved long cycles of analysis, decision-making, and execution. Businesses would collect data, analyze it, formulate strategies, and then implement them, often over the course of months or even years. In today's fast-paced markets, however, this approach is increasingly outdated. By the time a strategy is fully implemented, market conditions may have shifted, rendering the original plan obsolete.

AI offers a solution to this problem by enabling real-time analysis and decision-making. Instead of waiting for quarterly reports or annual reviews, businesses can now use AI to continuously monitor key performance indicators, market conditions, and competitor actions. This allows for strategies that are adaptive and responsive, changing dynamically as new data comes in.

For example, consider the logistics industry, where companies like FedEx and UPS are using AI to optimize their delivery networks. These companies are leveraging machine learning algorithms to predict package volumes, optimize delivery routes, and manage fleet operations in real-time. This enables them to respond immediately to changes in demand, traffic patterns, and weather conditions, reducing costs and improving service levels. In the future, this kind of real-time decision-making will become the norm across all industries, as businesses integrate AI into their core strategic processes.

Predictive Analytics and Proactive Strategy

One of the most exciting aspects of AI in the context of business strategy is its potential for predictive analytics. By analyzing historical data and identifying trends, AI can forecast future market conditions with a high degree of accuracy. This allows businesses to not only respond to changes but to anticipate them, crafting proactive strategies that give them a competitive edge.

In the automotive industry, for example, AI is being used to predict consumer demand for electric vehicles (EVs), helping manufacturers like Tesla, General Motors, and Volkswagen make decisions about production capacity, supply chain investments, and product launches. By using AI to analyze data on consumer preferences, regulatory trends, and technological advancements, these companies can stay ahead of market shifts, ensuring that they are positioned to capture growing demand for EVs.

This predictive capability is also transforming the healthcare industry. Pharmaceutical companies are using AI to predict the outcomes of clinical trials, identify promising drug candidates, and optimize supply chain operations. In doing so, they can reduce costs, speed up the time to market, and improve patient outcomes. In a world where markets are becoming more volatile and uncertain, the ability to anticipate change is invaluable, and AI is at the forefront of this transformation.

AI and Game Theory in Market Shaping

Beyond predicting market trends, AI and game theory are also being used to shape markets themselves. In many industries, the companies that succeed are not just those that respond to existing market conditions but those that actively shape the rules of the game. AI-driven platforms like Uber and Airbnb, for example, have reshaped entire industries by creating new business models and market structures that didn't exist before.

By combining AI and game theory, businesses can identify opportunities to influence market dynamics, creating conditions that favor their strengths and minimize their weaknesses. This could involve strategic partnerships, mergers and acquisitions, or even regulatory lobbying. The goal is not just to compete in the market but to shape the market in a way that maximizes long-term value.

For instance, companies in the renewable energy sector are using AI to model the impact of government policies, technological advancements, and consumer demand on the future of energy markets. By understanding these dynamics, they can position themselves as leaders in the transition to a low-carbon economy, influencing everything from energy pricing to infrastructure investments.

Ethical Considerations and the Role of Human Judgment

While the integration of AI and game theory offers tremendous potential for shaping business strategy, it also raises important ethical considerations. AI-driven decision-making can sometimes lead to unintended consequences, such as reinforcing existing biases or creating market distortions that harm consumers or smaller competitors. Additionally, as AI becomes more central to strategy, businesses must consider the role of human judgment and oversight.

One of the key challenges is ensuring that AI-driven strategies are aligned with broader societal goals, such as fairness, sustainability, and social responsibility. Companies will need to develop ethical frameworks for the use of AI, ensuring that it is not only used to maximize profits but also to contribute positively to society.

Moreover, human judgment will remain critical in areas where AI cannot fully capture the nuances of business strategy. While AI can process vast amounts of data and identify patterns, it cannot yet fully understand the complexities of human behavior, culture, or values. As such, the most successful businesses of the future will be those that combine the power of AI with human creativity, empathy, and ethical reasoning.

The Road Ahead: Embracing AI and Game Theory

As we look to the future, it's clear that AI and game theory will play an increasingly central role in shaping business strategy. The companies that succeed will be those that embrace these tools

, using them to create strategies that are not only more adaptive and precise but also more forward-thinking and proactive. Whether through real-time decision-making, predictive analytics, or market-shaping strategies, AI and game theory offer a new frontier for business leaders who are willing to challenge traditional assumptions and adopt a more dynamic approach to strategy.

The road ahead will also require businesses to navigate new challenges, from ethical considerations to the need for ongoing human oversight. By striking the right balance between AI-driven decision-making and human judgment, companies can unlock the full potential of these technologies, positioning themselves for long-term success in an increasingly complex and competitive world.

In the end, mastering the game of success in the future business landscape will require not only a deep understanding of AI and game theory but also a willingness to think beyond traditional strategies, embracing new possibilities and opportunities as they arise. Those who do will not just survive—they will thrive.

In today's rapidly evolving digital landscape, businesses face a constant threat of technological disruption. Entire industries can be transformed almost overnight by new technologies, making it essential for organizations to not only react but stay ahead of these disruptions. The convergence of technologies such as artificial intelligence (AI), machine learning, blockchain, the Internet of Things (IoT), and advanced analytics has fundamentally altered how businesses operate. These innovations not only bring opportunities but also significant challenges. If businesses do not actively engage with emerging trends and technologies, they risk being overtaken by more agile competitors.

Staying ahead of technological disruption is no longer just about adopting the latest tools or software. Instead, it requires a strategic and forward-thinking approach. Businesses must build the agility and resilience needed to anticipate change, understand how new technologies impact their industries, and, crucially, integrate these innovations into their long-term strategies. Companies that can successfully navigate this landscape will not only protect themselves from disruption but can become disruptors in their own right, reshaping industries and setting new standards.

The Challenge of Technological Disruption

The pace of technological change has accelerated exponentially in the past few decades. From the rise of personal computing to the development of the internet and mobile technology, businesses have continuously been forced to adapt. However, the disruptions occurring now are different. They are deeper, more interconnected, and occur at a much faster rate than before. AI, for example, is not just another technological tool—it represents a fundamental shift in how businesses make decisions, optimize processes, and interact with customers.

For instance, Kodak, once a dominant player in the film and camera industry, famously failed to anticipate the rise of digital photography. Despite having developed early prototypes of digital cameras, Kodak continued to focus on its traditional film business, assuming that digital would not replace film so quickly. By the time the company realized the magnitude of the disruption, it was too late, and Kodak filed for bankruptcy in 2012. This example underscores the importance of forward-thinking strategy. Businesses cannot afford to ignore emerging technologies or underestimate their potential impact.

Similarly, in the retail sector, companies like Blockbuster were blindsided by the advent of digital streaming services. Blockbuster was a market leader in DVD rentals but failed to recognize the potential of Netflix, which initially started as a mail-order DVD rental service. Netflix, however, embraced the internet's growing capabilities, transitioned to a streaming model, and ultimately redefined the entertainment industry. Blockbuster, which failed to evolve, became obsolete.

These cautionary tales illustrate how critical it is for businesses to not only monitor technological developments but also to build the flexibility needed to pivot when necessary. The key to staying ahead of disruption lies in understanding emerging trends and integrating them into a broader, long-term strategy.

Emerging Trends and Technologies That Will Redefine Strategy

While technological disruption is not new, the convergence of several groundbreaking trends will redefine business strategy in the coming years. Companies that recognize and harness the potential of these emerging technologies will have a significant competitive advantage. Here are some of the most important trends that businesses must pay attention to:

1. Artificial Intelligence and Machine Learning

AI and machine learning are already transforming industries such as healthcare, finance, manufacturing, and retail, and their impact will only grow in the future. AI has moved beyond simple automation and now includes capabilities such as predictive analytics, natural language processing, and deep learning, enabling businesses to make data-driven decisions and optimize processes at unprecedented speeds.

Consider how AI is reshaping the healthcare industry. AI-driven algorithms can analyze medical data to predict patient outcomes, assist in diagnosing diseases, and personalize treatment plans. For example, IBM's Watson Health uses AI to sift through massive amounts of medical literature and clinical data to provide physicians with insights and recommendations. This technology not only improves patient care but also reduces the time and costs associated with diagnosis and treatment planning. Healthcare providers that adopt AI are staying ahead of disruption by delivering more accurate, faster, and cost-effective care.

In the financial sector, companies are using AI to optimize trading strategies, manage risk, and detect fraud. JPMorgan Chase, for instance, has developed an AI system called COIN (Contract Intelligence), which reviews and interprets commercial loan agreements in seconds, a task that previously took legal teams up to 360,000 hours annually. This not only saves time and money but also reduces errors. AI's ability to analyze data and make decisions faster than humans enables businesses to operate more efficiently and profitably, creating a competitive edge for early adopters.

To stay ahead of disruption, businesses need to embed AI into their core strategies, using it not only to automate routine tasks but to enhance decision-making, predict future trends, and innovate faster than competitors.

2. Blockchain and Decentralized Systems

Blockchain technology, known for its role in powering cryptocurrencies like Bitcoin, is set to revolutionize industries beyond finance. Blockchain's core advantage lies in its decentralized, transparent, and secure nature, making it ideal for industries that require trust and verification without intermediaries.

In supply chain management, for instance, blockchain can provide a transparent and immutable record of every transaction, ensuring that goods can be tracked from origin to destination. This has enormous implications for industries such as food and pharmaceuticals, where traceability is critical for safety and compliance. Walmart, for example, has implemented blockchain to track the origin of its food products, reducing the time it takes to trace the source of contamination from seven days to just 2.2 seconds. This not only improves safety but also enhances operational efficiency, allowing Walmart to respond more quickly to food safety incidents.

Similarly, in the world of finance, blockchain has the potential to eliminate the need for intermediaries like banks and clearinghouses, drastically reducing transaction costs and settlement times. JPMorgan Chase has developed its own digital currency, JPM Coin, using blockchain to facilitate instant cross-border payments for its institutional clients. By leveraging blockchain, JPMorgan is staying ahead of disruption in the banking industry, where traditional payment methods are being challenged by faster, cheaper alternatives.

Businesses that fail to explore blockchain's potential risk falling behind as competitors adopt more secure, efficient, and transparent processes. Blockchain will become increasingly critical in industries that value security, privacy, and decentralized control.

3. The Internet of Things (IoT)

The Internet of Things (IoT) refers to the interconnectedness of everyday devices—from smart refrigerators to industrial machines—that can collect and share data. By 2030, it's estimated that there will be over 50 billion IoT devices globally. This explosion of connected devices is creating new opportunities for businesses to gather data, optimize processes, and create personalized experiences for consumers.

In manufacturing, IoT is driving the development of "smart factories," where machines, sensors, and systems are interconnected and can communicate with each other in real-time. General Electric (GE), for example, has developed its Predix platform, which uses IoT data from industrial machines to optimize operations, predict equipment failures, and reduce downtime. By integrating IoT into its strategy, GE is staying ahead of disruption in the industrial sector, where real-time data and predictive maintenance are becoming essential for competitiveness.

Retailers are also embracing IoT to create more personalized shopping experiences. Amazon's Echo devices, powered by its voice assistant Alexa, allow customers to shop, control smart home devices, and access entertainment simply by speaking commands. This seamless integration of IoT into consumers' daily lives is reshaping the retail landscape, with companies like Amazon leading the charge in redefining how people interact with technology.

For businesses to stay ahead of the IoT revolution, they must invest in connected technologies that allow them to gather and analyze real-time data. This data can then be used to enhance operational efficiency, predict trends, and deliver customized experiences to customers.

4. 5G and Advanced Connectivity

The rollout of 5G networks represents a quantum leap in connectivity, offering faster speeds, lower latency, and greater capacity than previous generations of wireless technology. 5G will enable real-time communication between devices, paving the way for advancements in autonomous vehicles, smart cities, and advanced robotics. This next-generation connectivity will also accelerate the adoption of technologies like AI, IoT, and augmented reality (AR).

In the automotive industry, for example, 5G will be essential for the development of autonomous vehicles. Self-driving cars rely on real-time communication with other vehicles, infrastructure, and cloud systems to navigate safely. With 5G's low latency, cars will be able to make decisions in milliseconds, dramatically improving the safety and reliability of autonomous driving. Companies like Tesla, Waymo, and Uber are already investing heavily in this space, understanding that the future of transportation will depend on the seamless integration of AI, IoT, and 5G technologies.

5G will also transform industries such as entertainment and gaming. With faster connectivity, consumers will be able to stream high-quality video, play immersive AR and virtual reality (VR) games, and experience real-time interactions with brands and media in ways that were previously impossible. For instance, Verizon is partnering with the NFL to provide 5G-powered augmented reality experiences for fans in stadiums, enhancing the live sports experience and creating new opportunities for engagement.

Businesses that invest in 5G technology will be able to deliver faster, more reliable services, stay connected to their customers in real-time, and innovate at a pace that slower networks simply cannot support.

5. Advanced Data Analytics and Personalization

Data is now considered one of the most valuable assets for any organization. However, the challenge lies not just in collecting data, but in analyzing it effectively to drive business decisions. Advanced analytics, powered by AI and machine learning, are enabling businesses to extract actionable insights from vast amounts of data, leading to more personalized customer experiences, optimized operations, and improved decision-making.

Take Netflix, for example. The company uses advanced data analytics to understand viewer preferences and behavior. By analyzing viewing habits, Netflix is able to recommend personalized content to its users, which keeps them engaged and reduces churn. This data-driven approach has been key to Netflix's success, allowing it to maintain its position as a leader in the highly competitive streaming industry.

In the retail sector, companies like Starbucks are using data analytics to personalize marketing campaigns and loyalty programs. By analyzing data from its mobile app and loyalty program, Starbucks can send personalized offers to customers based on their purchasing history, preferences, and even weather conditions. This targeted approach not only improves customer satisfaction but also drives revenue.

To stay ahead of disruption, businesses must invest in advanced analytics capabilities, using data to make informed, real-time decisions that cater to individual customer needs and preferences.

Building a Culture of Innovation and Agility

To successfully stay ahead of technological disruption, businesses must do more than simply adopt new technologies. They must build a culture that fosters innovation, agility, and continuous learning. This requires leaders to embrace change, encourage experimentation, and empower employees to take risks.

For example, Google's "20% time" policy, which allows employees to spend 20% of their work hours on projects that interest them, has led to the development of some of the company's most successful products, including Gmail and Google News. By giving employees the freedom to explore new ideas, Google has created a culture of innovation that helps it stay ahead of technological disruption.

Similarly, Amazon's relentless focus on customer-centric innovation has allowed it to stay ahead of competitors across multiple industries. Amazon constantly experiments with new technologies, from drone delivery systems to cashier-less stores, ensuring that it remains at the forefront of disruption in retail, logistics, and cloud computing.

Agility is also crucial. Businesses need to be able to pivot quickly in response to new opportunities and threats. This means adopting flexible organizational structures, using data to inform decision-making, and continuously refining strategies based on real-time insights.

The future of business is being shaped by an unprecedented wave of technological disruption. Companies that want to stay ahead must adopt a proactive, forward-thinking approach, leveraging emerging technologies such as AI, blockchain, IoT, 5G, and advanced analytics to create strategies that are not only resilient but also adaptive to the changing landscape. Building a culture of innovation and agility, where experimentation and continuous learning are encouraged, is key to staying ahead of the curve.

As technological advancements continue to accelerate, businesses that can anticipate disruptions, integrate new technologies into their core strategies, and remain flexible in their approach will thrive in the face of uncertainty. Those that fail to adapt risk becoming the next cautionary tale in an increasingly competitive and technologically-driven world.

APPENDICES

Appendix A: Key Concepts in Game Theory and AI Explained

In this appendix, we explore the foundational terms and concepts in Game Theory and Artificial Intelligence (AI) to provide a clear understanding for those looking to master the intersections of these powerful disciplines. This glossary serves as a quick reference guide to essential concepts that are pivotal for navigating the world of strategic business decision-making in the age of AI.

1. Game Theory

At its core, Game Theory is the study of strategic interactions among rational decision-makers. It assumes that individuals, companies, or entities, referred to as "players," are rational and make decisions that maximize their payoffs while considering the potential actions of other players. These interactions are modeled as games, where the "rules," "strategies," and "outcomes" are clearly defined. Game Theory provides a framework to analyze competitive situations, predict behaviors, and identify optimal strategies in various fields, from economics to politics, and now, increasingly in AI-driven business environments.

Key Terms:

- Nash Equilibrium: A situation in which no player can improve their payoff by unilaterally changing their strategy. In other words, every player's strategy is optimal, given the strategies of all other players. This is fundamental in competitive business scenarios, where companies seek a balance between cooperation and competition.

- Dominant Strategy: A strategy that results in a better outcome for a player, regardless of the strategies chosen by the other players. In a business context, this could reflect a company's decision to adopt a certain technology or pricing model that outperforms others regardless of what competitors do.

- Zero-Sum Game: A game where one player's gain is exactly balanced by another player's loss. In some industries, such as commodities trading, competition is fierce, and the market's total payoff is fixed, making strategic planning critical.

- Payoff Matrix: A table that illustrates the potential outcomes (or payoffs) of different strategies chosen by players in a game. This matrix is essential for visualizing strategic decisions in both competitive and cooperative business environments.

- Mixed Strategy: A situation where players randomize their choices rather than sticking to a single strategy. In AI-driven environments, this concept is particularly relevant for algorithms that incorporate randomness to predict outcomes or optimize decision-making under uncertainty.

2. Artificial Intelligence (AI)

AI refers to the creation of machines or algorithms that can perform tasks typically requiring human intelligence, such as learning, problem-solving, decision-making, and understanding natural language. In the context of business strategies, AI is increasingly being used to analyze vast datasets, predict market trends, optimize supply chains, and personalize customer experiences.

Key Terms:

- Machine Learning (ML): A subset of AI where algorithms improve their performance over time as they are exposed to more data. In business, ML is used to forecast market trends, detect fraud, and optimize customer segmentation. It's the backbone of many AI-driven strategies, helping companies refine their approaches based on real-time data.

- Neural Networks: A type of machine learning model inspired by the human brain's neural structure. Neural networks are used for tasks like image recognition, natural language processing, and autonomous decision-making. In business, they are crucial for advanced applications like AI-driven recommendation engines and predictive maintenance systems.

- Reinforcement Learning (RL): A type of machine learning where an agent learns by interacting with an environment, receiving rewards or penalties based on its actions. In Game Theory, RL is analogous to players learning optimal strategies through repeated play. In business, this is applied in areas like supply chain optimization, where the system learns from continuous feedback to improve efficiency.

- Deep Learning: A specialized form of neural networks with many layers (hence the term "deep") that allow machines to process data in a hierarchical fashion. Deep learning has revolutionized fields like image and speech recognition and is increasingly being used in business for analyzing complex data patterns, such as consumer behavior.

- Natural Language Processing (NLP): A branch of AI that enables machines to understand, interpret, and generate human language. Businesses leverage NLP for chatbots, sentiment analysis, and automated customer service, enhancing the way they interact with consumers and manage large volumes of unstructured data.

3. Game Theory Meets AI

The convergence of Game Theory and AI is transforming business strategies. By combining the predictive power of AI with the strategic insight of Game Theory, companies can model complex market dynamics, anticipate competitor moves, and devise strategies that are not only reactive but proactive.

- Multi-Agent Systems: In AI, multi-agent systems refer to environments where multiple AI agents interact, often modeled through Game Theory. These agents could be self-driving cars sharing a road or AI algorithms competing in a marketplace. Game Theory helps structure the interactions between these agents, optimizing collective outcomes or ensuring fair competition.

- Algorithmic Game Theory: A field that blends algorithms from computer science with Game Theory to solve problems involving strategic interactions in digital environments. This has significant applications in markets, online auctions, and ad placements, where companies leverage both AI and Game Theory to maximize returns.

- Cooperative vs. Non-Cooperative Games: In cooperative games, players can form alliances to improve their collective payoff, while in non-cooperative games, players act independently. AI can assist businesses in analyzing which approach would yield better outcomes depending on the competitive landscape.

4. Optimization and Decision Making

AI excels in optimizing complex systems, and when combined with Game Theory, it allows for better decision-making in competitive environments. Businesses can use AI to model various strategic scenarios, applying Game Theory to identify the best course of action in the face of uncertainty.

- Strategic Interaction in Markets: In financial markets or competitive industries, AI can analyze vast amounts of data, predicting how different players might act based on historical trends. Game Theory then helps in crafting strategies that consider these potential moves, allowing companies to remain agile and competitive.

- AI-Driven Auctions: Online platforms like Google and Amazon use Game Theory principles in their auction algorithms for ad placements. AI continuously refines these processes by analyzing how advertisers bid for space, ensuring that the most relevant ads are shown to the right users, maximizing revenue for both the platform and advertisers.

Appendix B: Case Studies of Game Theory and AI in Action

In this appendix, we present real-world case studies illustrating how Game Theory and AI are reshaping industries and driving success. These in-depth analyses provide practical insights into the application of these concepts in various sectors, highlighting their transformative potential.

1. Amazon: Optimizing Pricing Strategies with AI and Game Theory

Amazon is a prime example of a company that has mastered the art of dynamic pricing. By employing AI to track competitor prices, customer demand, and market trends in real-time, Amazon can adjust its prices to maintain a competitive edge while maximizing profits. However, it's not just the AI that makes this work—Game Theory plays a crucial role in modeling how competitors will respond to price changes.

Using a payoff matrix, Amazon can predict how a rival might react to a price drop or hike and adjust its strategy accordingly. This interplay of AI and Game Theory allows Amazon to dominate the e-commerce space, constantly staying one step ahead of competitors. The AI also considers consumer behavior, applying reinforcement learning to optimize not just pricing but the entire customer journey, from product recommendations to checkout processes.

2. Tesla: Self-Driving Cars and the Evolution of Multi-Agent Systems

Tesla's autonomous driving technology is a sophisticated example of multi-agent systems in action, combining AI with Game Theory. Each self-driving car acts as an agent, continuously interacting with other agents on the road—be it human drivers, traffic signals, or other autonomous vehicles. AI algorithms control each car's decisions, but Game Theory ensures that these decisions are optimized for safety, efficiency, and cooperation with other vehicles.

For instance, when multiple autonomous cars approach an intersection, Game Theory models help ensure that each car behaves in a way that maximizes overall traffic flow, while AI processes real-time data to make the most informed decision. This cooperation between AI and Game Theory is not only making driving safer but also pushing the boundaries of what multi-agent systems can achieve in real-world applications.

3. Google: Ad Auctions and Algorithmic Game Theory

Google's advertising platform is one of the most profitable AI-driven businesses in the world, and it heavily relies on Game Theory. The platform uses a Vickrey-Clarke-Groves (VCG) auction system, where advertisers bid for ad placement. This system, which is a type of second-price auction, ensures that advertisers pay only the amount needed to secure their spot, rather than the full value of their bid.

AI plays a critical role in refining these auction systems, analyzing billions of bids and user interactions to optimize outcomes. Google's algorithms predict how advertisers might behave in future auctions and adjust ad placements accordingly. Game Theory helps in designing the rules of the auction, ensuring fairness while maximizing Google's revenue. The constant interplay of AI and Game Theory makes Google's ad platform incredibly efficient, benefiting both advertisers and users.

4. Uber: Surge Pricing and the Balance Between Supply and Demand

Uber's surge pricing algorithm is another brilliant case where AI and Game Theory intersect. When demand for rides outstrips supply, Uber's AI detects this imbalance and increases prices to incentivize more drivers to get on the road. This dynamic pricing model is not only powered by AI but also grounded in Game Theory.

From a Game Theory perspective, Uber is solving a coordination problem. Drivers and riders are both players in the game, and the surge pricing algorithm is designed to reach an equilibrium where enough drivers are motivated to provide rides, while customers are willing to pay the increased fare. Uber's AI continually learns from each interaction, improving its predictive capabilities and ensuring that the surge pricing model remains efficient and fair.

5. Netflix: Personalization and Customer Retention Strategies

Netflix utilizes AI for personalizing content recommendations, but Game Theory plays a role in customer retention strategies. By predicting what content other streaming services might acquire or produce, Netflix can make strategic decisions about which shows or movies to prioritize. The company also uses Game Theory to analyze how competitors' actions—such as new content releases or changes in subscription pricing—might affect its user base.

AI enables Netflix to mine vast datasets of user behavior, helping refine its recommendation algorithm. Game Theory complements this by ensuring that Netflix's strategic content decisions are optimized, keeping users engaged and reducing churn. This interplay has been pivotal in Netflix's ability to stay ahead in the highly competitive streaming industry.

The merging of Game Theory and AI is not just a theoretical construct—it's actively transforming the way businesses operate across industries. From optimizing pricing strategies to revolutionizing customer experiences, the case studies above demonstrate how powerful these tools are in navigating the increasingly complex and competitive business landscape. By mastering these disciplines, businesses can not only keep pace with change but also proactively shape their futures, turning challenges into opportunities.

Appendix C: Resources for Further Reading and Learning

Mastering the intersection of Game Theory, Artificial Intelligence (AI), and business strategy requires a comprehensive understanding of both the theoretical foundations and the real-world applications of these fields. To help deepen your knowledge, this appendix provides an extensive list of recommended books, articles, and tools that offer insights into Game Theory and AI, with a focus on how these concepts are being applied to shape modern business strategies. Whether you're an academic, a business leader, or an aspiring strategist, these resources will equip you with the intellectual tools needed to navigate today's complex, AI-driven world.

1. Books on Game Theory

Books remain one of the best resources for gaining in-depth knowledge on a subject. Game Theory, with its rich mathematical foundations and real-world applications, has been explored by numerous scholars. Below is a list of essential books that provide a strong grounding in both the theory and application of Game Theory across various domains.

a) "The Art of Strategy: A Game Theorist's Guide to Success in Business and Life" by Avinash K. Dixit and Barry J. Nalebuff

This book offers a highly engaging and accessible introduction to Game Theory, with a particular focus on its application in business and everyday decision-making. Dixit and Nalebuff guide readers through the fundamental concepts of Game Theory—such as Nash equilibrium, dominant strategies, and mixed strategies—using real-world examples from politics, sports, and business negotiations. One of the strengths of this book is its focus on practical applications. For instance, it explains how businesses can use Game Theory to anticipate competitor actions and optimize pricing strategies.

Example: In one section, the authors explain how an airline can use Game Theory to decide whether to engage in a price war with a competitor. By anticipating the competitor's response to different price levels, the airline can choose a pricing strategy that avoids mutually destructive outcomes.

b) "Game Theory: A Very Short Introduction" by Ken Binmore

For those looking for a concise but rigorous introduction to Game Theory, Ken Binmore's book offers a compact yet comprehensive overview. This book distills the key concepts of Game Theory without sacrificing intellectual depth. Binmore focuses on both the mathematical underpinnings and philosophical implications of the theory, making it ideal for readers who are interested in a foundational understanding that bridges both economics and social behavior.

Example: Binmore uses the classic "prisoner's dilemma" to illustrate how Game Theory can apply to situations where individuals must decide whether to cooperate or act in their own self-interest, drawing parallels to real-world business negotiations and partnerships.

c) "Thinking Strategically: The Competitive Edge in Business, Politics, and Everyday Life" by Avinash K. Dixit and Barry J. Nalebuff

Another essential work by Dixit and Nalebuff, this book focuses on the strategic decision-making processes that business leaders must master. The authors use a combination of

Game Theory principles and real-world examples to show how individuals and companies can make better decisions by thinking several steps ahead.

Example: In discussing competitive strategy, the authors use examples from the fast-food industry, where companies must anticipate each other's menu pricing and promotional offers to maximize market share without eroding profitability. This is a direct application of Game Theory's emphasis on predicting competitors' actions and formulating counter-strategies.

d) "Games of Strategy" by Avinash Dixit, Susan Skeath, and David H. Reiley

This textbook is an excellent resource for anyone seeking a more formal and detailed understanding of Game Theory. It covers both the basic and advanced concepts, with a strong emphasis on real-world applications in business, politics, and economics. The book includes problem sets and case studies, making it particularly useful for students and professionals looking to apply Game Theory to real-world problems.

Example: The authors explore the "battle of the sexes" game to explain coordination games, where businesses must decide on mutually beneficial strategies, such as agreeing on industry standards for technology adoption.

2. Books on Artificial Intelligence

As AI becomes an integral part of modern business strategies, it is essential to understand the underlying technologies and their applications. The following books provide both technical and business-oriented insights into AI and its transformative potential across industries.

a) "Superintelligence: Paths, Dangers, Strategies" by Nick Bostrom

This book offers a deep dive into the future implications of AI, particularly the potential risks and rewards of achieving superintelligent machines. While it focuses on the broader ethical and existential questions surrounding AI, it is also a valuable resource for understanding the transformative potential of AI in reshaping industries, economies, and global competition.

Example: Bostrom explores scenarios where superintelligent AI systems could outcompete human businesses in strategy formulation, optimizing every aspect of operations from logistics to customer service in ways that are far beyond human capabilities.

b) "Artificial Intelligence: A Guide for Thinking Humans" by Melanie Mitchell

Mitchell's book is an accessible and engaging introduction to AI, covering the history, challenges, and future of the field. It is particularly valuable for readers who want to understand how AI works at a conceptual level, without getting bogged down in technical jargon. Mitchell covers the key AI technologies, such as machine learning and neural networks, and explains how they are transforming industries from healthcare to finance.

Example: Mitchell discusses how AI-driven systems like IBM's Watson have been used in medical diagnostics, applying machine learning to analyze vast datasets of patient records to recommend more accurate diagnoses and treatment plans.

c) "Prediction Machines: The Simple Economics of Artificial Intelligence" by Ajay Agrawal, Joshua Gans, and Avi Goldfarb

This book explores AI's impact on business decision-making, with a focus on how AI-driven predictions are transforming industries. The authors argue that AI essentially functions as a "prediction machine," providing companies with better tools for forecasting outcomes and making strategic decisions. This book is particularly useful for business leaders who want to integrate AI into their operations but are unsure of where to start.

Example: The authors use the example of ride-sharing platforms like Uber to illustrate how AI-driven algorithms predict demand and adjust prices dynamically, optimizing the balance between supply and demand in real time.

d) "The Master Algorithm: How the Quest for the Ultimate Learning Machine Will Remake Our World" by Pedro Domingos

In this book, Domingos explores the quest for the "master algorithm"—a single algorithm capable of learning any task. He takes readers on a tour of the different branches of machine learning, from decision trees to neural networks, offering insights into how these technologies are transforming industries. This book is particularly useful for understanding the various approaches to AI and their potential business applications.

Example: Domingos discusses how AI is being used in marketing to personalize customer interactions at scale, predicting which products or services individual customers are most likely to purchase based on past behavior.

3. Articles and Journals

In addition to books, articles in leading journals and business publications provide up-to-date insights into the latest developments in Game Theory, AI, and their applications in business strategy.

a) "The Dawn of Artificial Intelligence in Business Strategy" (Harvard Business Review)

This article explores how AI is changing the landscape of business strategy, from automating decision-making processes to transforming supply chains and customer engagement. The authors provide case studies of companies that have successfully integrated AI into their strategic planning, offering valuable lessons for other businesses looking to do the same.

Example: The article discusses how global retailer Zara uses AI to optimize its supply chain, using predictive analytics to forecast which products will be in demand and adjusting production schedules accordingly.

b) "AI and Game Theory in Business: The New Frontier" (MIT Sloan Management Review)

This article focuses on the intersection of AI and Game Theory, highlighting how companies are using these tools to navigate competitive markets. The authors explore how AI-powered systems are being used to simulate competitor behavior and develop strategies that maximize long-term profitability.

Example: The article features a case study on the airline industry, where AI and Game Theory are used to predict competitor pricing strategies, enabling airlines to adjust their prices dynamically and optimize profits.

c) "The Strategic Impact of AI on Business Models" (McKinsey Quarterly)

McKinsey's in-depth analysis of AI's impact on business models provides a comprehensive look at how AI is reshaping industries. The article covers the key ways in which AI is being used to enhance decision-making, improve operational efficiency, and create new business models. It is a valuable resource for business leaders looking to understand the long-term strategic implications of AI.

Example: The authors discuss how AI is enabling the rise of subscription-based business models, where companies use predictive analytics to anticipate customer needs and deliver personalized services on an ongoing basis.

4. Online Courses and Tools

In today's fast-paced business environment, continuous learning is essential for staying competitive. Online platforms offer a range of courses and tools for mastering Game Theory, AI, and business strategy. Below are some of the best resources available.

a) Coursera: "Game Theory" by Stanford University

This course, taught by Stanford University professors, provides an in-depth introduction to Game Theory, covering both its mathematical foundations and practical applications. It includes case studies and interactive exercises, making it ideal for business professionals who want to apply Game Theory to real-world challenges.

Example: The course includes modules on strategic decision-making in business, where students learn how to use Game Theory to optimize pricing strategies and negotiate more effectively with competitors.

b) edX: "Artificial Intelligence: Business Strategies and Applications" by Columbia University

This course offers a comprehensive introduction to AI, with a focus on its applications in business strategy. It covers key AI technologies like machine learning and natural language processing, and explores how these tools can be used to create competitive advantages in various industries. Participants will engage in case studies that illustrate the practical implementation of AI in real business scenarios.

Example: The course includes a section on how AI is transforming customer service through chatbots and virtual assistants. Students learn how companies like Sephora use AI-driven solutions to enhance customer engagement by providing personalized recommendations based on user interactions.

c) Khan Academy: "Introduction to Game Theory"

Khan Academy offers a free course that introduces the basic concepts of Game Theory in an easily digestible format. With video lectures and interactive exercises, this resource is perfect for beginners looking to understand the foundational principles of strategic thinking and decision-making.

Example: The course discusses the "prisoner's dilemma," a classic example used to illustrate the complexities of cooperation and competition, showing how these concepts apply to real-world scenarios such as business negotiations and competitive strategy.

d) Harvard Online: "Artificial Intelligence in Business"

This online program from Harvard focuses on the strategic implications of AI in the business environment. It covers critical areas such as ethical considerations, data management, and the integration of AI technologies into existing business models. The course is tailored for business leaders and decision-makers who wish to leverage AI for strategic advantage.

Example: The course emphasizes real-world case studies, such as how Netflix and Amazon use AI to personalize user experiences and enhance customer satisfaction, illustrating the power of data-driven strategies in today's marketplace.

5. Tools for Application

To apply the concepts learned from books, articles, and courses, business professionals can leverage various tools and software that incorporate Game Theory and AI. Here are some noteworthy options:

a) GAMS (General Algebraic Modeling System)

GAMS is a high-level modeling system for mathematical programming and optimization. It is widely used in industries for modeling complex systems and decision-making processes that can be analyzed through Game Theory. GAMS allows users to formulate and solve problems involving linear, nonlinear, and mixed-integer programming.

Example: Businesses in logistics can use GAMS to optimize supply chain decisions by modeling the interactions between different stakeholders, applying Game Theory principles to identify the best outcomes for all parties involved.

b) MATLAB

MATLAB is a powerful programming platform used for mathematical modeling, data analysis, and algorithm development. It has a range of toolboxes that can be used to apply Game Theory models and algorithms for simulations and strategic decision-making in business contexts.

Example: Companies can use MATLAB to simulate market conditions and competitor behaviors, allowing for the analysis of different strategic scenarios and the development of optimal business strategies.

c) R and RStudio

R is a programming language and software environment for statistical computing and graphics, widely used among data scientists. R and its integrated development environment, RStudio, offer packages specifically designed for Game Theory analysis and machine learning applications, making it a versatile tool for businesses.

Example: Analysts can use R to conduct simulations based on Game Theory models, analyzing how different strategies would play out in various market scenarios. R's capabilities for data visualization can also help communicate findings to stakeholders effectively.

d) Google Cloud AI and Machine Learning Tools

Google Cloud offers a suite of AI and machine learning tools that businesses can use to implement predictive analytics, natural language processing, and other AI capabilities into their operations. These tools facilitate the integration of AI into existing business processes, enabling companies to enhance their decision-making and customer interactions.

Example: A retail business can use Google Cloud's machine learning tools to analyze consumer behavior data, allowing for personalized marketing strategies that align with predicted purchasing patterns.

6. Professional Organizations and Online Communities

Engaging with professional organizations and online communities is an excellent way to stay updated on the latest developments in Game Theory, AI, and business strategy. These platforms often provide valuable networking opportunities, workshops, and resources.

a) The Game Theory Society

This international organization is dedicated to fostering the study and application of Game Theory. The society organizes conferences, publishes research, and provides educational resources. Engaging with the Game Theory Society can help professionals stay at the forefront of research and applications in this field.

Example: Members of the society can access exclusive research papers and participate in annual conferences, where they can share insights and collaborate with leading experts in Game Theory.

b) The Association for the Advancement of Artificial Intelligence (AAAI)

The AAAI promotes research and education in artificial intelligence. By joining this association, members can access a wealth of resources, including research publications, conferences, and workshops focused on the latest AI developments.

Example: The AAAI hosts an annual conference that gathers AI professionals from academia and industry, providing a platform for networking and knowledge sharing.

c) LinkedIn Groups and Online Forums

LinkedIn and online forums like Reddit have numerous groups and discussions focused on Game Theory and AI. Engaging in these communities allows individuals to ask questions, share experiences, and gain insights from other professionals in the field.

Example: Joining groups such as "Game Theory & Decision Science" on LinkedIn can facilitate discussions about the latest trends in Game Theory applications in business, allowing members to exchange ideas and strategies.

7. Podcasts and Webinars

Podcasts and webinars have become increasingly popular as a means of consuming knowledge on-the-go. Here are some notable options that focus on Game Theory, AI, and their implications in business strategy.

a) "The AI Alignment Podcast"

This podcast explores various aspects of AI, including its ethical implications, future risks, and how AI can be aligned with human interests. The discussions often touch on Game Theory principles in relation to AI development, making it a valuable resource for understanding the strategic implications of AI.

Example: Episodes feature interviews with leading researchers who discuss how Game Theory can help manage the strategic decisions around AI deployment and safety protocols.

b) "Game Theory 101"

This podcast is an excellent resource for those looking to understand Game Theory concepts in a straightforward and entertaining way. The host discusses various Game Theory applications and explains complex ideas in an accessible manner.

Example: One episode explores how Game Theory can explain why people cooperate in business settings, providing practical insights for leaders seeking to foster collaboration within their organizations.

c) "The Business of AI" Webinar Series

Hosted by various business schools and organizations, this series of webinars covers a range of topics related to AI in business, including strategies for implementing AI technologies and case studies of successful AI applications.

Example: A recent webinar discussed how major companies have successfully integrated AI into their supply chain management, highlighting the role of Game Theory in optimizing these strategies.

Conclusion

In summary, mastering Game Theory and AI in the context of business strategy requires continuous learning and engagement with a variety of resources. The books, articles, courses, tools, and organizations outlined in this appendix provide a robust framework for understanding and applying these critical concepts. By immersing yourself in these resources, you can develop the strategic mindset needed to navigate the complexities of today's business landscape and leverage AI and Game Theory for competitive advantage.

Whether through formal education or self-directed learning, the journey to mastering these fields will equip you with the knowledge and skills necessary to thrive in an increasingly interconnected and data-driven world.

END